B'day pressie
from Tina
10.01.87.

Modern
ASTROLOGY

Modern ASTROLOGY

by

ANN HENNING

ROBERT HALE · LONDON

© *Ann Henning 1983 and 1985*
First published in Swedish 1983
English edition first published 1985

Robert Hale Limited
Clerkenwell House
Clerkenwell Green
London, EC1

Henning, Ann
  Modern astrology.
  1. Astrology
  I. Title
  133.5   BF1708.1

ISBN 0-7090-2362-6

Photoset in Times by
Kelly Typesetting Ltd,
Bradford on Avon, Wiltshire
Printed in Great Britain by
St Edmundsbury Press, Bury St Edmunds, Suffolk
Bound by WBC Bookbinders Ltd

Contents

CONTENTS

CONTENTS

For maximum benefit

Part One of this book gives you a comprehensive introduction to astrology and its application in modern life. Part Two contains a large amount of reference material which will enable you to interpret astrological charts for yourself and others. Until recently, such interpretation was available only through skilled astrologers, as it necessitated complex calculations. Nowadays, however, these calculations can be done by computer and, as you will find in this book, casting a horoscope need not be more difficult than consulting a dictionary or an encyclopaedia. We recommend that you take advantage of the specially developed MODERN ASTROLOGY DATA SERVICE to obtain your personal astrological data. With that information at hand as you read the book, you can use your own case to test and verify the various astrological concepts, and at the same time acquire a fresh aspect on your character and situation in life. You can also, of course, ask for details of other persons.

If you want to know more about personal relationships, you can ask for a so-called synastric or comparative analysis, which compares your birth-chart to that of another person. This interpretation will reveal just how well you are suited to one another and how the relationship affects either of you, for better and for worse.

A sample of the print-out you receive from the data service can be seen on page 94. Complete instructions how to use it appear in Part Two.

Each set of data will cost you £2, but the charge for four sets is only £6.

For personal astrological data, to be interpreted with the help of this book, send the following information to MODERN ASTROLOGY DATA SERVICE, P.O. Box 683, London SW10 9TA, and enclose your postal order or cheque made payable to MODERN ASTROLOGY DATA SERVICE.

1 Name of the person.
2 Address to which you want the details sent.
3 Date of birth.
4 Time of birth (the more accurate, the more specific the analysis. If time is unknown, give it as 12 noon).
5 Place of birth – be specific.
6 Type of analysis wanted – personal or comparative or both? For a comparative analysis enclose details for both persons as above.
7 Enclose payment: £2 for each analysis, personal or comparative. For each four analyses requested at any one time, the charge is £6.

FINALLY, ENSURE THAT YOUR INFORMATION IS COMPLETE.

In memory of
David Heneage

PART ONE

General information

1 Astrology – what can it do for you?

Do you believe in it?

On learning that I've studied astrology, most people ask me the same question: Do you believe in it?

I have no ready answer to that. Astrology to me is not a matter of faith. I don't think it should be. Its greatest benefit comes if you look upon it rather as a language to clarify and express things which would otherwise be difficult to put into words. A tool to be used, not a creed.

There are other, more relevant questions, which I can answer with the conviction brought on by years of practical experience: Does it work? Can astrology make life easier, happier, richer? Yes, it does work. It does help you make life easier, happier, richer, whatever you like.

What can it do for you?

More specifically, what can astrology do for you? What direct help does if offer?

When properly applied, it gives you a chance to get to know your true self, to reach the essence of your own being.

Most people find that the identity shown by the horoscope is verified by their own experience and self-knowledge. It's not a coincidence that most people have such an instinctive fondness for their own chart, including any flaws it may reveal.

If you can identify your strengths and weaknesses, you're in a much better position to control your personal development. Shortcomings can be dealt with to the point where they no longer affect you, and assets can be fully and deliberately exploited. You may find obstacles in areas where you had hoped to go further – but you are just as likely to discover a promising potential which you haven't yet had the opportunity or confidence to pursue.

By pointing out the best chances of development, astrology gives everyone a chance to flourish.

Personal freedom

It's a general misconception that astrology is deterministic. This is not so. Rather than curtailing your personal freedom, it actively encourages the exertion of free will: by providing a balanced picture of the person you really are and showing the motivations behind your normal responses, it makes you much better equipped to take independent decisions, avoiding the pitfalls presented by impulsive or erratic behaviour. It's only when you know yourself that you're at liberty to choose what course to follow.

Freedom is necessary for self-realization and fulfilment in life, those coveted things which elude so many of us. And yet a lot of people disclaim that freedom – feeling that they are safer stuck in the narrow rut assigned for them. Then there are those who are so intent on making their way in the world that they lose sight of the personal happiness and peace which at heart they long for. Others again are so dejected by suffering or failure that they are unable even to try to make the most of their own possibilities.

Astrology tells you how to tackle such difficulties, first of all by pointing them out to you, then leading you to the root of your problems. When you see them clearly enough to understand them, the solution shouldn't be far away.

As long as your problems and their causes are unknown to you, they will keep you trapped, and personal freedom will be forever beyond your grasp. Only awareness can break these fetters and give you a chance to make of life exactly what you want it to be.

Such awareness is afforded by astrology.

Relationships

It's an additional comfort to see one's problems in relation to those of other people, to find that everyone has to suffer from time to time and that every life is a matter of give and take. Astrology shows that life is surprisingly fair: we all have periods when we thrive and flourish, when we bide our time and when we have to follow suit. Each chart has its favourable and its troublesome aspects, which are activated with the same regularity for all people.

The astrological perspective helps you understand not only your own failings but also those of others. By explaining the basis of other people's behaviour, astrology increases your tolerance of their limitations as well as your appreciation of their qualities.

It also shows you that each interhuman relationship brings out specific mutual responses in the persons involved: you find someone evasive, they find you persistent. You call someone stingy, they call you extravagant. You see someone as vulnerable, they see you as protective.

There is an astrological method systematically to compare two horoscopes and so assess just what dynamic energies – constructive or destructive – are brought out by that combination. In close relationships, such insight can be of immense value and save everyone concerned considerable emotional wear and tear.

The future

Moving over to the more doubtful area of speculation into the future, you may ask how astrology here can be used in a credible manner, without depending on an element of faith.

One basic assumption has to be made: that there is a time and a place for everything; that it is possible and desirable carefully to time decisions and actions for the best results. Some people feel instinctively when the time is right. Astrology confirms and increases this awareness, teaching you to go along with the tide rather than lose yourself in a vain struggle against it.

Certain planetary constellations are traditionally supposed to correspond to specific circumstances on Earth. Some are better suited than others for different activities.

A person who has learnt the method will usually find that the circumstances for any dramatic interlude in his previous life will agree with those suggested by traditional astrological concepts. In any case, it is always possible to discern a regular pattern for the course of someone's life: each time the planets assume certain positions, he/she experiences the same flow of good luck, excitement, havoc, depression or whatever the case may be. This knowledge suggests what the future holds: 'Christmas twelve years ago was the happiest time of my life. Those conditions will repeat themselves next summer – I'm already looking forward to it.' Or: 'Five years ago I went through a difficult period – but it led to much better conditions all over and I would never have wanted to be without it. In two years' time a similar situation will develop – but this time round I'll know better how to handle it.'

Generally speaking, *trends* in a person's life, as opposed to *events*, are easy and safe to foretell. They are also easy to confirm, since most people can tell straight away whether they are going through a favourable, confusing, tedious or demanding period. Astrology gives you the timing of such periods, preparing you for what's to come and reminding you that nothing lasts for ever.

Newspaper horoscopes

For many people, astrology is represented by the horoscopes published regularly in newspapers and magazines. Some read them with blind faith, others are sure they are written by some editor without any astrological knowledge, formulated in such general terms that they would apply to anyone.

The newspaper horoscopes are certainly generalized, but they are not pure conjecture. Few journalists would have sufficient imagination to compose twelve different forecasts day after day, year after year, without running the risk of repeating themselves.

On the other hand, horoscopes in the press often contain factual errors; forecasts are entered for the wrong day or month or sign.

But there is a more serious criticism of the horoscopes we see in newspapers and magazines: they can be harmful for those who read them, if they suggest that life is a matter of chance and so indirectly discourage people from taking responsibility for themselves and their actions.

A skilled, conscientious astrologer can, however, write

explanatory and meaningful horoscopes. These can also be complemented by readers' columns where astrologers give personal advice in reply to letters. But first of all, the press will have to learn enough about the subject to take it seriously.

The professionals

When sensibly used, astrology is not the mysterious and, to many people, frightening occult science it has been made out to be since time immemorial. Unfortunately, there have always been people with a vested interest in keeping the subject shrouded in magic. Many fortune-tellers still rely on astrology rather than a crystal ball. But this use of astrology belongs to an era when fate was recognized as the main force in human life; when man was seen as a victim of capricious gods rather than an independent rational creature with a free will and both the right and a duty to shape his own destiny.

Luckily, a new breed of astrologers is beginning to emerge. They have adjusted their skills to suit life in modern society. They act mainly as advisers or consultants, combining their astrological knowledge with psychological training. They help clients understand their problems and suggest means to overcome them, pointing out their best potential assets and possible ways to realize them.

Astrology as therapy

In a therapeutic situation, astrology can be used along with other psychological methods: it reflects objectively the background of psycho-social patterns, showing these mechanisms as a link between the individual and society as a whole. Limiting the amount of introspection and increasing social awareness often bring better results than endless soul-searching.

Another considerable advantage is the fact that astrology is very well suited for self-therapy. Most of us need assistance in sorting out ourselves and our lives now and then, but only a few get as far as a professional therapist. And even those who do consult a professional astrologer/therapist benefit more if they first study their own chart.

Astrology by computer

Until recently, special mathematical skills were required for drawing up an astrological chart. The long, complicated calculations are perhaps the main reason why the subject has always been so inaccessible to laymen. Today, however, we are helped by modern technology: all astrological data can be produced by computer, which also makes them more accurate, eliminating miscalculations and sources of error. To interpret these data, you need no more than a basic knowledge of the astrological principles and their function. That knowledge is provided in Part One of this book. Part Two is mainly for reference: it comprises a large number of listed interpretations, some of which will apply to you personally.

There are astrological tables (the so-called ephemerides) published to enable people to produce their own data, without having to rely on a computer. The ephemeris shows the day-to-day position of each planet. If you are prepared to learn the method, which is rather complex, both the ephemerides and handbooks teaching the method are included in the list of suggested reading on page 240.

For beginners, the computer method provides a good gateway to astrology. It enables you to get familiar with individual horoscopes without first having to spend a lot of time on technical studies.

2 Astrology yesterday

Primitive man

It can't have taken primitive man very long to discover that his life was affected by atmospheric conditions. The most obvious relationship was of course that between Sun and Earth, which made him sleep at night and wake up in the morning, freeze in winter and sweat in summer.

When man started to till the soil, he soon realized that the best results were achieved if sowing and reaping were done with the Sun and Moon in certain positions. Once he added the fact that the crop ought to be adjusted to existing soil conditions, he had established a philosophical foundation for astrology: the outcome of each measure taken on Earth depends on events taking place in the Universe, but can be manipulated by man to improve the end result.

Some hundred, or thousand, years later, man turned his eye to the planets, those bright spots in the sky which, unlike the fixed stars, moved in a regular pattern, each one in its own rhythm. Some of them passed over the firmament in a matter of weeks, whereas others took years to describe the same passage. Consequently, the quicker-moving planets occasionally caught up with the slower ones, to spend a shorter or longer period in the same place.

Man in his close relationship with nature took note of this. He paid particular attention to the sky at times of great success or appalling misfortune, and found that there was a connection between the appearance of the firmament and the pattern of his own life. Such information was handed down from one generation to another: Man was still fighting for his survival and needed all the assistance available to him. During the course of centuries, the knowledge became more specific and could finally be formulated as general principles. A symbolic language was developed to describe life on earth in relation to the cosmic environment.

Ancient cutltures

In the cultures that we call the world's oldest, astrology was already well established. As far as we know, the Chaldeans in Mesopotamia were the first to make exact observations and calculate the planetary motion, from about 3000 BC. Some ten horoscopes from the fifth century BC still exist on tablets in cuneiform.

Although life among the Chaldeans was strongly affected by astrology, they interpreted the archetypal symbols to fit in with their strictly patriarchal system. Astrology was confined to matters of state, and astrologers were statesmen and councillors to the king. It never reached out to the individual, who was of little importance in the Chaldean social structure.

The same can be said about the older dynasties in Egypt, where the kings had their burial chambers and the lids of their sarcophagi adorned with pictures of the stars. It was the Egyptians who divided the day into twenty-four hours – although the length of the hours varied – and the year into 365 days and twelve months with thirty days in each. The constellations and the Zodiac, on the other hand, were taken over from Chaldeans and Greeks.

The Bible contains a number of allusions to astrology and its principles. In the Old Testament, in Ecclesiastes (3:1–5), we find the following well-known verses:

> To everything there is a season,
> and a time to every purpose
> under the heaven;
> a time to be born,
> and a time to die;
> a time to plant,
> and a time to pluck up
> that which is planted;
> a time to kill,
> and a time to heal;
> a time to break down,
> and a time to build up;
> a time to weep,
> and a time to laugh;
> a time to mourn,
> and a time to dance.

Another, even better-known example, from the New Testament, is the star of Bethlehem and the three wise men who were, obviously, star-gazers.

'Know thyself' was one of the ancient Greeks' mottoes. Greek philosophy held the individual in great esteem, and it's not surprising that the Hellenes were the ones to develop the individually orientated astrology as a means to increased self-knowledge. They gave us the word 'astrology', which means simply 'star knowledge'. They counted seven planets in the solar system and named the days of the week after them. Many Greek personal horoscopes have been preserved.

During the Hellenistic era (the second century AD), when the Greek culture spread to the rest of the ancient world, astrology flourished in India, Persia, Egypt and the Roman Empire, each country taking over the symbols but interpreting them to suit their own social system. The mundane Romans, for example, focused their interest on predictions regarding worldly status. They had coins stamped with star signs, which they happily spent among the numerous, not always genuine astrologers who marketed their services in almost every forum. The Romans gave us the Latin names, which we still use for the starsigns.

Ptolemy, active in Alexandria in the second century AD, has been called the father of classical astrology. His main contribution was to compile and record the ancient astrological concepts in a major work called the *Tetrabiblos*. It is difficult to tell exactly how much of Ptolemy's work was original, but it seems likely that much of it was based on earlier Greek writings, which in turn had been inspired by the Chaldeans.

The works of Ptolemy and other Hellenic writers were in due course translated into Arabic and preserved by the Arabs during the Dark Ages. The Arabs, with their interest in mathematics and strong fatalistic beliefs, found it easy to adopt astrology as part of their faith.

Europe

Towards the end of the Middle Ages, interest in astrology was again aroused in Europe. The beautifully illuminated and

23

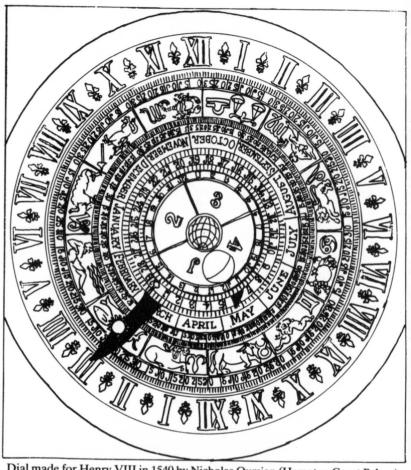

Dial made for Henry VIII in 1540 by Nicholas Oursian (Hampton Court Palace).

illustrated 'books of hours' often show the symbols of the Greek Zodiac. From the fourteenth century onwards, ornamental clocks depicting the motion of the different heavenly bodies became a common feature of European cathedrals and town halls. One example can be seen in Strasbourg Cathedral and another late but splendid one at Hampton Court Palace near London.

With the Renaissance, classical ideals were reinstated, and with them, the Greek emphasis on the individual. This paved the way for a renewed interest in the humanistically inclined astrology. It was taught as a major subject at most universities and mastered by most scholars. Pope Julius II even based the time for his coronation on the position of the stars.

New scientific discoveries at this time did not lessen the credibility of astrology. When the Polish astronomer Copernicus launched his theory that the planets revolve around the Sun, this was the beginning of a revolution as far as astronomy (the strictly scientific study of space) was concerned, but in no way did it affect the astrological concept. Astrological observations are made from Earth and seen as relative to the Earth. Astrology has never pretended to make objective observations of space. It simply maintains that certain phenomena on Earth correspond to certain phenomena in the Universe – *as seen from Earth*. It aims to *reduce* the immense scale of the Universe to human proportions – not the other way round.

Copernicus' heliocentric theory (Sun at the centre) was, incidentally, not new. The Greek astronomer Aristarchus had formulated this idea as early as the fourth century BC. Then, as in the Renaissance, astrologers agreed that, even if it were scientifically correct, it would not make any difference to their work.

In the sixteenth century, astrology was the domain of the cultured and highly educated and an accepted part of life at the royal courts. Shakespeare's plays contain over a hundred references to the 'influence of the stars'. Romeo proclaims: 'Here will I . . . shake the yoke of inauspicious stars from this word-wearied flesh', and in *King Lear*, the Duke of Kent declares: 'It is the stars, the stars above us, govern our conditions.' In *Julius Caesar* we read: 'The fault, dear Brutus, is not in our stars but in ourselves, that we are underlings.'

This was also the time of the great court astrologers. Tycho Brahe was appointed by the Danish royal family. He built the first observatory in the modern sense of the word, the 'Uranienborg' on the island of Hven, now in Sweden, the ruins of which still remain. Brahe, using both Ptolemy's and Copernicus' systems, gathered a huge amount of empirical data, based on his own precise observations. He compiled ephemerides (astrological tables) which he used to make predictions. Many of these were political, and some turned out to be stunningly accurate. With the astrologers' strong position at the royal courts, astrology had again become state-orientated.

Brahe spent his last years in Prague, working with the German astronomer Johannes Kepler as his assistant. Kepler was another court astrologer, employed by the Emperor Rudolf II, who took a keen interest in the subject. But Kepler was more absorbed by the scientific aspects. He realized that the ephemerides set up by Brahe left a lot to be desired. After many years of research he discovered that the planets do not move in concentric circles, as had been assumed until then, but in elliptic orbits. Once he had established the real orbit of each planet (Kepler's laws), exact ephemerides could, for the first time in history, be compiled.

For his observations Kepler used the telescope which had been introduced by his contemporary Galileo. Between them Kepler and Galileo developed the Copernican system and managed to prove that the heliocentric theory was correct.

In the seventeenth century astrologers were still busy trying to predict social events. The Englishman William Lilly was highly acclaimed for the accuracy of his predictions, such as the tragic fate of Charles I and the Great Fire of London. But the very accuracy occasionally landed him in trouble: after the fire he was accused of complicity, and it was only his previous record of reliability that had him acquitted.

The interest in astrology at this time was great, but so was the interest in witchcraft and magic. It is understandable that the uneducated masses found it difficult to distinguish between the various mysterious forces which were thought to govern their lives. Astrology became more and more confused with superstition. And when the eighteenth century came, with its theories of enlightenment and rationalism, astrology was strictly separated from astronomy. The latter was accepted as an exact science in full agreement with the rational spirit of the day, whereas the former was condemned as folly.

It is interesting to note that only the people who had taken the trouble to study the subject still supported it. Sir Isaac Newton, whose work *Principia* of 1687 was of paramount importance to the natural scientists of the time, was himself a convinced astrologer – something which baffled his more ignorant contemporaries.

In parts of Europe, Britain in particular, astrology went through a temporary boom during the romantic Victorian era. Alan Leo was a popular astrologer whose most important works were published around the turn of the century and retained their relevance almost until present times.

The twentieth century on the whole has taken the stance of the 'enlightened' sceptical rationalism of two hundred years ago. An encyclopaedia dating from 1929 rejects astrology as 'mystical fantasies' and compares it with determinism. The following judgement concludes the entry:

> These days, astrology is to be regarded mainly as an outdated form of superstition. However, this does not mean that it is altogether extinct. In many countries, England and America in particular, there are societies counting thousands of members who defend the ancient astrological doctrine. Usually, these followers also support the sickly spiritualism of Emanuel Swedenborg.

This was written some fifty years ago. During the decades that have since passed, the world has seen a technological explosion of incredible dimensions. We have now reached a level where technology by far exceeds the narrow limits of the rational mind. And, once again, man has been forced to accept even that which his mind cannot conceive. At the same time, the advanced technology seems to be bringing us closer to the scientific explanation of the astrological principles. Astrology is facing its second Renaissance.

3 Astrology today

Modern society

The historical exposé shows that each culture has adjusted astrology to fit in with its own social structure. As society has changed, so have the application and interpretation of the astrological concept. The most interesting aspect of astrology is perhaps the ease with which it lends itself to infinite adaptation. Its symbols are so basic, so archetypal, so unaffected by philosophy and ideology, that they have moved unchanged through hundreds and thousands of years and a number of highly different civilizations. The only thing that has changed, that has been in a state of constant transformation throughout, is the way people have chosen to interpret them.

In historical terms, our modern society has developed very quickly. Philosophy and spiritual life have not quite followed its pace. Nor has our attitude to astrology: some of the interpretative patterns of old times still linger on, although they have little to offer people today. The best example of this is the fortune-telling aspect.

Perhaps modern people have a secret desire, some primordial instinct left as a remnant in our genes, to abandon themselves to something they call fate; to denounce the responsibilities conferred on them by democracy, justice and equality and imagine that the outcome of their lives has nothing to do with them but is determined by forces beyond their control. A convenient theory – but using astrology to justify this kind of escapism is not using it to its best advantage.

We have created a society where the demands on the individual are higher than ever before, where the call for personal success is imperative, and man has nothing but his own merits to fall back upon. The monster of our times is not fate but failure.

The compensation for all our struggle is the chance of true

self-realization. If we can achieve that, the pain and suffering inevitably connected with our enforced personal growth will have been worthwhile. And this is where we need guidance. We need a framework anchored outside our personal and social entanglements, a framework that can help us develop our individuality for its own sake, not just exploit it in response to demands and pressures.

This framework is the main function of astrology in modern society.

A science?

The new kind of astrology is most concerned with describing the individual, his life and his social rôle. It is therefore to be regarded as a social science, closely related to psychology. The modern humanistic astrology was, incidentally, founded by Carl Jung, who is better known for his pursuits in the field of psychoanalysis.

More doubtful is the link between astrology and natural science. In ancient times, all science was based on observations and conclusions deducted from experience. Astrology – like behavioural science – still works this way, whereas the natural sciences today accept only that which can be fully explained and objectively proved. Since we haven't yet got far enough to explain the reasons behind the astrological functions, astrology does not qualify as a natural science. But there are signs that this may well change in the face of advancing technological development.

The latest technology, with its emphasis on electro-magnetism and cybernetics, stresses the interdependence between the different components in a system. The link between the Universe and certain natural phenomena on Earth is well documented. In *The Sea* (1951), in her description of the tidal movement, the American marine biologist Rachel Carson states that a force of gravitation exerts an attraction between each drop of sea water and each star in the universe. It seems logical to suggest that a similar power connects each cell of the human body to the planets of the solar system: the microcosm to the macrocosm. After all, we carry the primaeval sea within us – the main constituent of

our bodies is water. And every atom of our anatomy origi-
nated in the stars, billions of years ago.

Rachel Carson goes on to declare that the cosmic power
controlling the tidal waves is situated far beyond the Earth
and is impartial in its function, i.e. exerting the same strength
all over our planet. The local variation of the tides, on the
other hand, depends on differences in topography. In other
words, each drop of sea water is affected by the same cosmic
power, but it manifests itself in different ways in different
places, due to varying geographical conditions.

In the same way, an astrologer would add, we are all subject
to the same cosmic influences, but since we are all different,
our responses to them vary.

Not only the sea water, Carson continues, is under the
influence of this power. Many living organisms seem to
depend directly on the tidal movement to survive. But it has
been found that the tidal waves do not rule the lives of these
organisms. If, for example, a colony of the sea worm
Convoluta is transferred to an aquarium in a laboratory,
hundreds of miles from the sea, the worm still continues to
describe the movements which in the sea would have coincided with the rhythm of the tides. The tides and the worms
are affected by a parallel stimulation, coming from space.

Astrology and genetics

The great genetic sensation in the 1960s which led to the
awarding of a Nobel Prize in Chemistry was the discovery of
the so-called 'genetic code'. This is founded on the concept of
DNA (deoxyribonucleic acid), a basic substance present in all
living cells. The structure of the DNA molecule is extremely
complex, and its possibilities of variation are infinite. The final
formula is unique to each individual of the human species. It
hasn't yet been established exactly what forces determine its
composition, but it is not unlikely that the cosmic forces
prevalent at its formation could have an effect.

The DNA code has verified what astrology has alleged but
not managed to prove for thousands of years: that each
individual is born with a predetermined potential which

decides not only his basic characteristics but also his destiny (which is *not* the same thing as fate).

Modern genetic scientists have been called 'the prophets of our time', because of their ability to make scientifically exact predictions. In the USA, a method has been devised to test genetic matter with the aim of identifying a person's strengths and weaknesses, primarily on a physical basis. Geneticists are now able to predict future health hazards, from skin cancer to blood clots and schizophrenia. They have also found a link between physical characteristics and patterns of behaviour.

Someone may voice the objection that astrology can't possibly be compared with genetics, since the two contradict each other. Genes are inherited from the parents, whereas astrological features (in so far as they exist) come about by chance.

As a matter of fact, astrology and genetics confirm each other. Astrological characteristics are inherited just like the genetic ones. This is easy to prove: if you compare the horoscopes of the members of one family, there will be a high rate of repetitions which can't possibly be coincidence. In some families, one generation is born after another with the same unlikely and unusual astrological feature or constellation appearing and reappearing throughout. It's a fascinating exercise to go through the horoscopes of your close relations, to assess from whom your various traits have been inherited. Usually most can be found with either parent, but in some cases you have to go further afield, to grandparents or great-grandparents.

If you think about it, it's only logical that people should procreate and give birth to their offspring at times when the atmospheric conditions are compatible with their own character. The moment may not be chosen deliberately, but nature's timing of pregnancies and births is less capricious than it appears.

Relatively often you find that a child is born with a chart that is a paraphrase of that of its father or mother. It happens, for example, that a parent who possesses a certain potential but lacks the faculty to realize it has a child with the same aptitude, coupled with the ability to develop it. This seems to suggest that the parent is intended to prepare and support the

31

child who has been given the task of giving practical application to their joint talent. It is also common that women give birth when the Sun, Moon, Venus or the Ascendant is in exactly the same position as in their own or the child's father's chart. Such links usually make for a close connection between parent and child.

Astrology and the world

The idea that we are all products of our environment is a fairly modern one. But astrology has always maintained that our character is a reflection of the world we were born into, that our future development is determined by conditions surrounding us at birth. People born in the middle of a raging war normally have aggressive traits, those born under tragic circumstances tend to be melancholy, and those born in great happiness usually grow up to be harmonious.

All this can be deduced without the aid of astrology. But without some kind of perspective, the world picture as well as the immediate environment can be difficult to assess objectively. We all know that it is easy to be wise after the event, and that any social process becomes much clearer when seen through the lens of history.

Astrology provides a similar perspective – but the distance is made up of space rather than time. The universal conditions – that is, conditions affecting each and every entity in the Universe, including ourselves – are the same for each given moment. The planets are subject to the same forces as the world and its inhabitants. The planets themselves have no effect on our lives; that's only simplified astrological terminology. But their positions and internal relationships reflect our own situation; studying them is rather like seeing ourselves and our environment in a huge magnifying mirror.

If we look long enough into this mirror, we shall find that in each life there are periods when our personality is most perfectly expressed, when our existence is most complete and destiny lies within reach. With astrology we can increase our awareness of these times of fulfilment, anticipate them before they happen and dwell upon them afterwards. We can extend them infinitely and make sure they always live within us, bridging time and space.

At the same time, there is the world around us. We are all part of the same system, and whether we like it or not, we put our stamp on it, influencing our environment for better or for worse. Just as our thoughts, feelings and actions at each moment of our life are affected by conditions surrounding us, these thoughts, feelings and actions reach out to the world and contribute to change its face.

This is where the free will comes in. By overruling the forces we're subjected to and controlling, first of all our inner life, making it what we want it to be, we can also influence our circumstances and make them what we want them to be.

That art is perhaps the most important thing we can learn from astrology.

4　The solar system

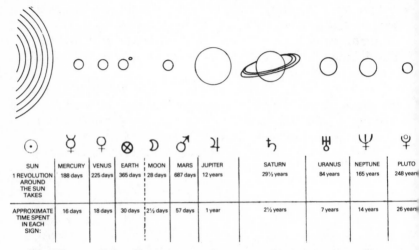

	SUN	MERCURY	VENUS	EARTH	MOON	MARS	JUPITER	SATURN	URANUS	NEPTUNE	PLUTO
1 REVOLUTION AROUND THE SUN TAKES		188 days	225 days	365 days	28 days	687 days	12 years	29½ years	84 years	165 years	248 years
APPROXIMATE TIME SPENT IN EACH SIGN:		16 days	18 days	30 days	2½ days	57 days	1 year	2½ years	7 years	14 years	26 years

The Moon and the planets in our solar system with their relative positions and orbits around the Sun. The Moon's orbit is around the Earth. Below the line is the approximate time spent by each planet in one sign.

Above the name of each planet is shown its symbol. The symbols are the 'shorthand' figures used in tables and charts all over the world, understood by all astrologers. The symbols are made up of three different basic elements: the circle, the semi-circle and the cross – the ancient metaphysical symbols of spirit, soul and matter.

⊙　*The Sun*'s symbol is the circle: that which is without beginning and without end, the perfection of the Universe. The dot in its middle stands for the personal fate or the glimmer of life. Generally, the Sun symbol expresses the complete individual potential.

☽　The crescent of *the Moon* – the semi-circle – shows the soul, the unconscious reflection of the spirit within us. The Moon represents the blind spot in man where he remains a child throughout life. Thus the Moon is associated with spontaneous, instinctive responses.

☿　*Mercury* is one of three planets, whose symbol includes all three figures: on top the semi-circle, resting on the circle, under which is the cross. This is a reflection of man's intellectual capacity and awareness: mind over matter.

♀ *Venus* has as its symbol the circle over the cross: the triumph of spirit over matter, whilst the symbol for *Mars* ♂ shows the spirit expressing itself through matter: the cross has here been converted to an arrow, rising from the base of the circle.

♃ *Jupiter*'s symbol shows the individual soul connected with the material world: but the crescent is striving up from the cross of matter in an attempt to reach higher.

♄ *Saturn*'s symbol shows the material world as superior to the individual soul. The cross of matter above the crescent. The principle of the flight of time (Saturn in Greek is Chronos, i.e. time). A reminder that the world remains when the individual soul passes.

♅ The principle of *Uranus* is the cross of matter on top of the circle, surrounded by two straightened semi-circles: a potential circle, using matter as its medium. This symbol shows the sudden awakening of the soul to spiritual awareness. Uranus represents intuition and receptivity on an abstract conscious level.

♆ The symbol for *Neptune* is the semi-circle lying above the cross of matter and penetrated by it: another version of the soul's struggle to free itself of the fetters of the material world. It can also be seen as the material world finding a sublimated expression through the individual soul.

♇ The symbol for *Pluto*, incorporating all three functions, shows the individual soul raised above the material level, and in its 'bowl' the liberated spirit floats freely. The symbol represents the spiritual death and regeneration within man. (In the USA another symbol is used: ♇ , simply a contraction of the initials of Percival Lowell, the man who officially discovered Pluto, and the first two letters in the planet's name.)

The picture also gives an idea of the relative size of each planet. Mercury and Pluto are the smallest (apart from the

Moon), Venus and Earth are about the same size, Saturn is quite a large planet and Jupiter the largest of them all.

In the picture you can see how long it takes each planet to revolve once around the Sun. The orbit takes longer to complete the further you get from the Sun, because the orbit becomes longer and the Sun's gravitation weaker with greater distance. To our eye it looks as if the outer planets move more slowly across the sky.

The Moon, being a satellite of Earth and not a planet, moves most quickly of all: it completes its passage across the sky in only twenty-eight days.

Of the planets, the innermost planet, Mercury, is the fastest, followed by Venus, Earth, Mars, Jupiter, Saturn, Uranus, Neptune and Pluto in that order. Their speed varies considerably – Mercury completes its course in 188 days, while Pluto takes 248 years to describe one revolution.

The Earth's cycle is 365 days – that is, one year. By definition, one year is the time it takes the Earth to revolve around the Sun. But in astrology all observations are made from Earth, and therefore we call this the Sun's passage across the firmament. The way we see it from Earth, the Sun takes one year to move around the firmament's horizon. (The vertical passage, due to the Earth's rotation round its own axis, takes, of course, twenty-four hours.)

The figures at the bottom of the picture show how long each planet stays in each sign of the Zodiac. Again, the Moon is at one end of the scale with only 2½ days in each sign. Mercury spends an average of sixteen days and Pluto from fifteen to thirty-five years in each sign.

Seen from the Earth, certain planets sometimes seem to change direction. This is an optical illusion, when Earth in its orbit around the Sun moves away from a planet. The latter appears to go in reverse, and the phenomenon is called *retrograde motion*. This has some significance to the interpretation. Retrograde planets, in charts marked with R, indicate more introverted functions.

Each time a planet occupies your birthsign it will affect you in one way or another. Due to the variation of their different rhythms, the intervals of each planet vary considerably.

The Moon comes back to you every twenty-eight days, but

Pluto only once in 248 years. In between we have planets like Jupiter and Saturn, occupying your birthsign every twelve and twenty-nine years respectively.

Generally speaking, the faster a planet moves, the more superficial its influence, and equally, the slower the planet, the more profound the effect. The Moon, for example, relates to moods, and Mercury to intellect – things which change easily and frequently. Neptune, on the other hand, rules your subconscious and Pluto your social attitudes – things which take many years to alter.

In astrology, the planets are divided into three different groups. The first, with the Sun, Moon, Mercury, Venus and Mars, contains the *personal* planets, mainly appertaining to our character and individual pursuits. The second group consists of Jupiter and Saturn and relates to our *social* function: our ability to adjust to a system, a social structure, rules and regulations, also within ourselves. The third group, finally, is made up of Uranus, Neptune and Pluto, planets of *transformation*. They rule profound inner development in relation to social changes – major developing processes which can extend over decades.

The planets

Each planet and the Sun and Moon are traditionally ascribed certain characteristics. If you make yourself familiar with the character of each planet, you will be in a good position to understand the interpretation of the Zodiacal signs and the effect each planet may have on your person and life:

⊙ The Sun is at the centre of the Universe, the main heavenly body, the life-giving power, the core of our existence. The Sun stands for your general attitude to life, your inner being, your personality, your free will, your conscious character, your potential and – hopefully – its realization. It represents warmth, creativity and generosity, activity and vitality. It helps you express your deepest intentions.

Without the Sun our identity would be lost – the other planets are just there to complement it.

As we become more mature, the potential of the Sun in our

horoscope develops towards the most sincere, purposeful and well-considered form of self-realization. The Sun enlightens and stimulates different aspects of our life at different times, strengthening our ego on different levels. It orientates itself in the present.

☽ The Moon, on the other hand, symbolizes your reactions – the instinctive, impulsive, early acquired side of your psyche. It determines your temperament and your need for security – both formed during infancy and strongly influenced by the relationship with the parents. Sensitivity, receptivity, trust and emotional responses all come under the Moon, as well as your roots, origin and background; in brief, your past. The Moon represents change and fluctuation within a fixed framework, for example your moods within the bounds of the temperament.

The tides, the growth of crops and women's menstrual cycle are some well-known examples of the effect of the Moon in nature. Children's character is determined by the position of the Moon in their chart.

☿ Mercury stands for the mind: thoughts, ideas, intellect, verbal expression, versatility, dexterity and intelligence. Mercury is never more than one sign away from the Sun on either side and should work together with the Sun and other planets to lend depth and meaning to the mind. By itself, Mercury, with all its curiosity, wit and gaiety, achieves little of permanent value and soon becomes restless and superficial. Its verbal ability can also be abused for lying and deceiving.

Mercury represents communication on all levels. The brain, senses and nervous system come under this planet.

♀ Venus symbolizes love and affection, beauty and art, balance and harmony, pleasure and social life, good taste and style. She is never more than two signs away from the Sun on either side and should always be supported by the Sun and other planets. With no other motivation than her own gratification, Venus becomes spoilt, lazy, pleasure-seeking and decadent. Properly used she does, however, emerge as a charming, popular and sociable creature. Venus detests anything ugly, shoddy and sordid and will soon be broken down by such conditions.

♂ Mars is the energy-bringer, and his action is either constructive or destructive. He stands for heroism, dynamic action, initiative, independence and enthusiasm. At the same time, however, he represents impatience, irritation, anger, strife, dispute, aggression, cruelty, war and destruction. Violence and accidents partly appertain to Mars. Our desires and cravings – in particular the sex drive – plus the manner in which we express them are determined by Mars.

The presence of Mars tends to speed up processes, but it can also urge us to activity for no good reason, without tangible results. If Mars (i.e. anger and frustration) is suppressed for too long, the consequences may be drastic.

♃ Jupiter symbolizes benevolence, aspirations, expansion, development, judgement, values, wisdom and philosophy. History, foreign countries and languages, travel, religion, literature, law and higher education are all referred to Jupiter, which is understandable, since they were originally academically related. Jupiter is generous on both the material and spiritual level. That thing called 'luck' is usually his doing. On the other hand, we don't always keep the gifts bestowed upon us under Jupiter – they tend to appear as flying opportunities, whereas permanent success calls for more than just good fortune.

The other side of this planet shows hypocrisy and insincerity. Opportunities may be lost through carelessness, neglect, waste and bad judgement. There is also a lack of moderation, and his over-optimism has been many people's downfall, especially in the field of gambling.

♄ Saturn stands for responsibility, duty, discipline, organization, diligence, security and dignity. A serious, sober planet, but not devoid of good intentions. Saturn behaves just like a good, strict and just parent in ensuring that each person gets exactly what he deserves. He delays processes, teaches us difficult lessons, challenges our patience and puts us to severe tests, sometimes to the limit of our endurance. But if we pass the tests, our reward is sure to be forthcoming, and the rewards of Saturn are worth more than anything Jupiter could ever come up with. Saturn gives nothing for nothing – but his gifts are for keeps. He helps us – or forces us – to reap what we have sown. If we have mismanaged life in the past, we may suffer during his visits, but when all is said and done, Saturn leads us to our lasting achievements.

♅ Uranus is a modern planet, representing our individuality, which in extreme cases turns us into eccentrics, rebels or renegades. Teenage crises are one reflection of Uranus, and so are all extreme groups in conflict with the established society. In his right context, Uranus gives an enormous creative potential which could border on genius. People who care for a comfortable life and like to hide behind the protective barrier of social rôles and patterns greatly fear the effects of Uranus, which they experience as infinitely traumatic. The planet has a tendency to awaken us – often brutally – from our secure, complacent everyday existence and show us a more truthful picture of ourselves and our life situation – something of which we might have preferred to remain ignorant. The only way out of a Uranian confrontation is to go forward, to develop and change. There is no way back.

One thing you can rely on with this planet around: it won't be dull. And despite things like divorce, violence and accidents, one must respect the planet's intention: to provide us with the courage to be ourselves. The personal freedom that Uranus forces on us in the long run is well worth all the shocks he puts us through.

♆ Neptune is the planet of illusion and as such mystical, immaterial, spiritual, elevated and sublime. He is also untidy, other-worldly, unrealistic and disorganized. The planet rules charm, dreams, imagination, inspiration and genius, directing our attention to things beyond the material world. As a higher octave of Venus, he incites the love that goes beyond the senses and personal needs, that is based on charity, sympathy, mercy and compassion. Neptune has great reserves of altruism, idealism, humanity and humility.

At the same time, though, this can be a dangerous planet, inducing states of confusion, misunderstandings, deception and lies, mental disturbance, escapism and self-destruction.

Without Neptune, life would appear humdrum and trivial. It is he who lifts the soul high above Earth's futilities and gives us hope when all else fails.

♇   Pluto is a secretive, explosive planet – forceful and trans-
forming, his function indicating deep-going changes and a
transformation process based on the principle of spiritual
death and regeneration. Pluto also stands for mass involvement and politics and reaches out to society in a constructive
or destructive manner. Another facet of his compelling nature
is an attraction to power struggle, not only in politics but also
in finance and sex – all considerable power factors in today's
society. Pluto brings out tension and contradiction and
conflict, within man or in society, in extreme cases leading to
total destruction. His force is most positive when the tendency
to eliminate is brought under control and used to make way
for spiritual or social re-birth.

If you stop for a moment and reflect on the character of
each planet – with which planet or planets do you feel an
affinity? Which comes or come closest to what you see as your
true identity? Make a note of your choice. Later on you'll be
able to see whether this planet is strongly represented in your
chart.

5 The Zodiac

The Zodiac was originally related to the constellations of stars placed like a band along the celestial Equator. The astrology practised today mainly subscribes to the so-called Tropical Zodiac, based on the Earth's passage around the Sun and the climatic seasons that ensue: spring, summer, autumn and winter. The astrological year always begins when the Sun enters the sign of Aries (the Spring Equinox). Approximately once every 26,000 years, the Tropical Zodiac coincides with the constellations which gave the signs their names. Some 2,000 years ago, the spring equinox (Aries 0°) coincided with the constellation of this name.

Due to an astronomical phenomenon called the precession of the Equinoxes, the Spring Equinox slowly moves backwards through the sign constellations, spending approximately 2,200 years in each sign. The sign it occupies gives the name to the so called astrological *age*.

At present we are in the process of leaving the age of Pisces and entering the age of Aquarius.

When an astrological chart is drawn up and interpreted, it is based on the Spring Equinox at 0° Aries, followed by the other signs in the order they have in the Tropical Zodiac, each one occupying 30°, or a twelfth of the celestial Equator.

Looking at the planets from Earth, we see each planet projected against the background of the horizontal band of stars. It will fall within the boundaries of one or other of the twelve different sections. This is what we mean when we talk of a planet occupying a certain sign.

When you say you were born under one of the signs, you really mean that you were born at the time of year when the Sun occupied that particular starsign. At different times of the year, we see the Sun rise and set in different places along the horizon. That is because it is moving through the different signs. Unlike the planets, the Sun always occupies the same starsign at the same time each year – that is not surprising if you remember that our definition of 'a year' is based on the Sun's passage over the sky. The Sun enters Aries around 20 March, Taurus around 20 April, Gemini 20 May, Cancer 21 June, Leo 22 July, Virgo 22 August, Libra 22 September, Scorpio 23 October, Sagittarius 22 November, Capricorn 21 December, Aquarius 20 January and Pisces around 19 February.

On the day you were born, each of the eight planets plus the Sun and Moon occupied one or other of the twelve signs. You probably know already what sign the Sun was in – that is, your Sunsign, or birthsign. As you go on to interpret your horoscope, you will take into account not only the position of the Sun but also that of the Moon and the eight planets.

The distribution of the planets shows great variation. In some cases, a person is born with all eight of them and the Sun and Moon in different signs. But it is more likely that two or more of them form a conglomeration in one of the signs. If three or more planets are gathered in one sign, this is called a *stellium*. When that happens, the characteristics normally associated with that particular sign will be strongly represented in your personality.

This is part of the explanation why some people are more typical representatives of their Sunsign that others, and why descriptions of the Sunsign seem more accurate in some cases that others. It also explains why two people born on the same day but in different years can be totally unalike. If several planets occupied a sign different from your Sunsign when you were born, they will balance the influence of the Sun – perhaps even conceal it. On the other hand, if you have both the Sun and several planets in the same sign, you should find that you have most of the characteristics attributed to that sign.

The Western school of astrology sets the Sunsign first, the sign of the Moon second and the Ascendant, the sign rising on the horizon at the moment of birth, as number three. Indian astrology sees the Moonsign as the most important, whereas Chinese astrology is based on a cycle that coincides with that of Jupiter. But each horoscope is affected to a larger or lesser extent by the position of each one of the eight planets after the Sun, Moon and Ascendant.

43

The planetary positions, their signs and their internal relations are constantly changing. Because each planet has an orbit and a rhythm of its very own, the astrological picture changes every day – every minute, even, if you really see to the details. No day is like any other. No pattern is ever repeated.

The Zodiac on paper

If you stand on Earth (which I suppose you do) and look up at the sky, it appears rather like the inside of an immense inverted bowl. Reduced to two dimensions and a human scale, this would be a circle with the Earth in the middle. On paper, therefore, the Zodiac is usually depicted as a circle

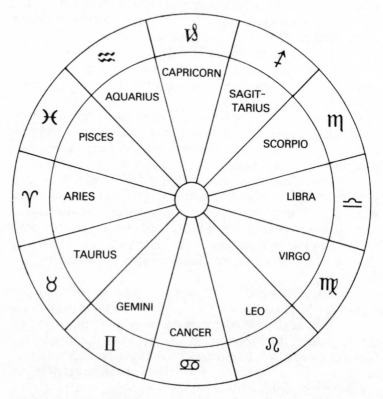

A graphic version of the Zodiac, showing the signs and their symbols.

(360°) divided into twelve equal sectors of 30° each: the twelve signs.

On a map reflecting the sky as seen from Earth, the directions are naturally reversed compared to an Earth map, just as in a mirror. East is therefore to the left, west to the right, south above the horizon and north below. The eastern horizon runs from the centre point (that is, Earth) to the left (east). This is the starting-point of the Zodiac, just as the sun rising on the eastern horizon marks the beginning on the day. The twelve signs are then counted counter-clockwise from this line.

The astrological year traditionally starts with the spring or the vernal equinox around 21 March, when day and night are of the same length and the Sun passes over from the sign of Pisces to Aries. Therefore, the Zodiac is always depicted with the eastern horizon as the dividing-line between Pisces and Aries, and Aries as the first sign underneath it. The second sign is Taurus, the third Gemini, and so on, counter-clockwise.

We are now talking about the Zodiac as an independent unit, without relation to the Sun or any planet, or to any horoscope. If you learn the intrinsic characteristics of each sign, this will make the interpretation of your chart easier.

At the end of each circle sector you can see the symbol of that particular sign. Just like the planetary symbols, these appear in the astrological tables and charts.

♈ is the symbol of Aries, showing the horns of the ram. ♉ is Taurus, the head of the bull, with smaller horns. ♊ stands for the twins, that is, Gemini, and ♋ shows you the claws of the crab, Cancer. ♌ is reminiscent of the lion's mane, Leo. ♍, the symbol for Virgo, is like a letter 'm' ending in a loop. Libra is symbolized by ♎, rather like scales, and Scorpio has an 'm' like Virgo, but this one ends in an arrow, the sting of the Scorpionic tail: ♏. Sagittarius the archer is symbolized by an arrow (what else?) with a cross-bar: ♐, and Capricorn has a letter 'v' with a loop: ♑, not very goat-like. Aquarius the water-carrier has two waves, ♒, and Pisces, finally, has the symbol ♓, showing two stylized fishes joined by a cross-bar.

45

Rulers

Each sign of the Zodiac is traditionally said to be *ruled* by one or two of the planets or the Sun or Moon. If you know the *ruler(s)* of a sign, it's easier to understand what it signifies, since the rulers colour and help identify the nature of their respective signs. It is also worth remembering that a planet when it appears in the sign it rules becomes extra powerful, its energy manifesting itself more easily and typically when it falls in its own sign.

Most signs have only one ruler, but some have two, as you can see in the picture opposite. Mercury, Venus, Mars, Jupiter and Saturn each rule two signs; the other planets and the Sun and Moon rule only one each.

The rulers are a theoretical help to define the character of each sign and should not be confused with the position of the planets in the horoscope.

Sign division

In our attempt theoretically to identify the character of each sign, we have other aids beside the planetary rulers. There is a traditional method of division, placing the twelve signs in different groups of varying size. This method of grouping gives us a deeper understanding of the function of each sign and the energy it sets in motion. For interpreting a horoscope it is invaluable.

The origin of the method is not quite certain, but it was recorded and used by Ptolemy in Alexandria in the second century AD. Since then it has been employed by all genuine astrologers in the West.

Duality

First of all, the signs are divided into two main groups, *positive* and *negative*. Every other sign, beginning with Aries, is said to be positive, and every other from Taurus onwards is said to be negative. This designation is strictly objective and does not imply any kind of evaluation.

The positive signs are also called *masculine* or *conscious*, whereas the negative signs are *feminine* or *instinctive*. The masculine/feminine terminology can be misleading, since

SYMBOL SIGN	NAME OF SIGN	NAME OF RULER	SYMBOL PLANET
♈	ARIES	MARS	♂
♉	TAURUS	VENUS	♀
♊	GEMINI	MERCURY	☿
♋	CANCER	MOON	☽
♌	LEO	SUN	☉
♍	VIRGO	MERCURY	☿
♎	LIBRA	VENUS	♀
♏	SCORPIO	PLUTO	♇
♐	SAGITTARIUS	JUPITER	♃
♑	CAPRICORN	SATURN	♄
♒	AQUARIUS	URANUS	♅
♓	PISCES	NEPTUNE	♆

Key to the Zodiac: Rulers in their respective sign/s and symbols.

different cultures have different ideas of the typical behaviour of each sex. The distinction has an Oriental origin and is comparable with the Chinese Yin and Yang principle.

Generally, one could say that the Western World tends to overestimate the value of the positive, masculine, conscious charge, which has an outgoing, executive, future-orientated, uninhibited, self-motivating and active force, geared towards *expressing impulses from within*.

The East attaches greater significance to the negative, feminine, instinctive charge, which is introverted, reflective, passive, contemplative and cautious, geared towards *receiving impressions from outside*, often from the past.

It's wrong to think that the negative signs should be less capable than the positive ones – the difference is the fact that the former calmly await their opportunity, whereas the latter go out and create their own.

A well-balanced chart should have an equal representation of positive and negative signs. A surplus of *positive* signs gives

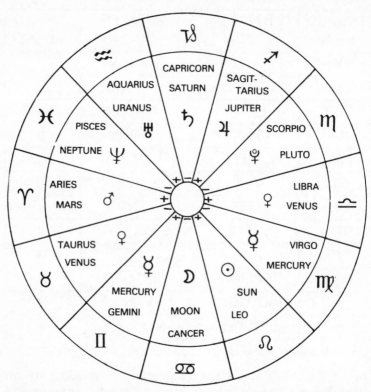

Positive and negative signs. The picture illustrates the chart on page 47. The positive signs, marked with +, are Aries, Gemini, Leo, Libra, Sagittarius and Aquarius. Negative signs, marked with −, are Taurus, Cancer, Virgo, Scorpio, Capricorn and Pisces.

us a person who involves himself personally and intensely, often in creative projects with a good constructive purpose. He consumes his energy as soon as it is produced, which means that he lacks reserves. In the same way he spends his money at the rate it comes in. People like this are very active but, because they never rest, they run a risk of burning themselves out. If they overexert themselves, recuperation takes a long time. Demands from other people and everyday trivialities tend to weigh them down, and they get harassed in a crisis. They risk being egotistic, superficial, insensitive and inconsiderate.

A surplus of *negative* planets make a person shy, perhaps

furtive, and introspective. He is very dependent on having security. The main driving force is his reaction to external influences: needs, habits, emotions, inhibitions. People like this are prepared to make sacrifices. They also have great resources to summon when necessary. They are hard-working, with great endurance and thrift; they like to accumulate possessions. Crises don't seem to affect them much – except that they tend to flourish under difficult conditions. They accept a mundane life and can become very narrow and limited in their outlook. Their personal development is often frustrated.

If you find that you have a surplus of either kind, you ought to search for points of balance in your chart to develop consciously. Many artists have a surplus of negative signs (providing depth of emotion), with perhaps one single positive point of balance. This then becomes the channel for their talent: the practice of it becomes their safety-valve. In the same way, people with mainly positive signs and the odd negative point of balance will find that this is their one source of rest, peace and revival.

Qualities

The signs are also divided into three groups with four signs in each, the three different *qualities*. Qualities are also called *modalities* or *ways of functioning*, which will give you an idea of their significance.

The qualities are *cardinal* (fundamental), *fixed* (stable) and *mutable* (flexible). A sign's quality tells you how its intrinsic energy manifests itself.

The *cardinal* signs set the world in motion – without cardinal initiative everything would come to a standstill. Their reactions are direct and immediate but can be rash and ill-considered. Cardinal signs *generate* energy; they like to tackle new projects but don't always conclude them; results are not a primary concern for them. They soon become restless and impatient and are often busybodies, seeing constant activity as a purpose in itself. This breeds opportunism. *Cardinal* people are usually articulate but can be abrupt. They have high metabolism, jerky movements, a lean and sinewy build and sharp features.

The *fixed* (stable) signs, on the other hand, *concentrate* energy. They ensure that the world remains and develops along established, long-term lines. Without anticipating events, they add one brick to another, slowly and purposefully, until a structure of permanent value has been erected. *Fixed* signs do not change their opinions or values; compromise is not for them. Often they have to struggle harder than others, but their achievements are outstanding, and they keep the result of their efforts throughout life. They are patient and determined but can also be slow, torpid, stubborn, obstinate and dogmatic. They don't like changes. *Fixed* people look determined and often have a strong, square jaw, a heavy build and an upright carriage. Their movements are poised.

Cardinal initiative and fixed determination together make for an enormous capacity, but they wouldn't get far, were it not for a third factor: *mutable* adjustment and direction.

The *mutable* (flexible) signs administer the gathered experience of the world and apply it; they *distribute* energy to ensure that it finds an appropriate outlet, avoiding friction and promoting harmony. The mutable signs are like oil between the wheels; they are excellent go-betweens. A deficit of mutable signs makes for difficulty in understanding people and processes, so that a lot of valuable energy will be misdirected. A surplus of these, on the other hand, breeds passivity, weakness of character and inconsistency. Such people have to make a supreme effort to achieve lasting results. They are most attracted by existing conditions – ambitions and objectives come second. Their greatest success comes in fields where they act as catalysts: brokers, agents, etc. Mutable people tend to have soft features and gesticulate more than others.

When dealing with the different signs, remember that *cardinal* signs need relaxation, *fixed* signs stimulation and *mutable* signs moral support.

A sound balance between the qualities is always to be preferred. If you have a marked imbalance in your chart, you should try to compensate for it by external measures and conscious efforts. Different signs of the same quality are often at odds with each other.

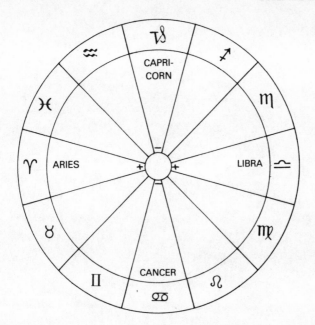

Cardinal signs.

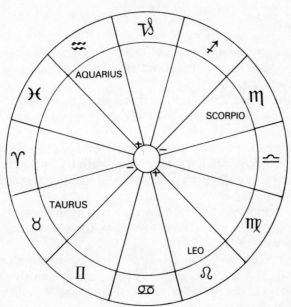

Fixed signs.

51

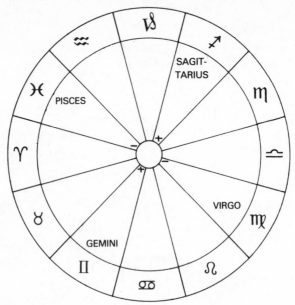

Mutable signs.

Elements

The third grouping of the signs is the *elements*. There are four of them – fire, earth, air and water – with three signs in each, one of each *quality*.

The three fire signs and the three air signs are all positive, whereas the three earth signs and the three water signs are all negative.

The elements show your *personal means of expression:*

Fire employs action, courage, warmth, wholehearted enthusiasm, vitality, passion, self-assertion, sincerity and general exuberance.

Earth employs common sense, practicality, caution, a realistic sense, material comforts, sensations and attention to physical well-being.

Air employs clarity of thought, logic, concepts, ideas and objective theories, tolerance and the spoken or written word. Thoughts are formulated and communicated rather than applied in practice.

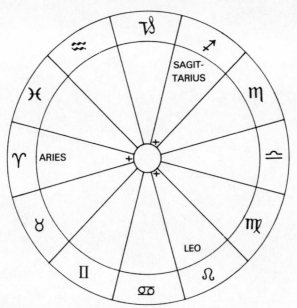

Fire signs.

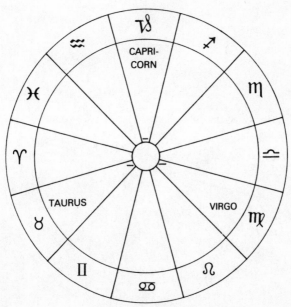

Earth signs.

53

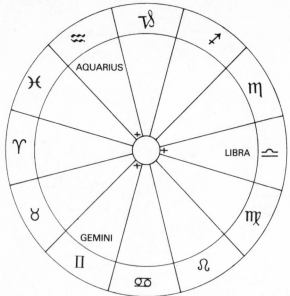

Air signs.

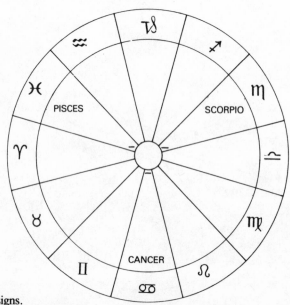

Water signs.

Water employs sensitivity, self-preservation, imagination, artistic talent, sympathy, compassion, idealism and charity.

Fire should be met with calm, *earth* with generosity, *air* with loyalty and *water* with firmness.

The two *positive* elements, *fire* and *air*, support and favour each other. So do the two *negative* elements, *earth* and *water*.

The elements should be evenly distributed in a chart. A surplus of any one of them is a problem:

Too much fire makes a person self-centred, impatient, restless, impulsive, arrogant, thoughtless and insensitive.

SYMBOL SIGN	NAME OF SIGN	QUA-LITY	QUALITY	ELEMENT
♈	ARIES	+	CARDINAL	FIRE
♉	TAURUS	−	FIXED	EARTH
♊	GEMINI	+	MUTABLE	AIR
♋	CANCER	−	CARDINAL	WATER
♌	LEO	+	FIXED	FIRE
♍	VIRGO	−	MUTABLE	EARTH
♎	LIBRA	+	CARDINAL	AIR
♏	SCORPIO	−	FIXED	WATER
♐	SAGITTARIUS	+	MUTABLE	FIRE
♑	CAPRICORN	−	CARDINAL	EARTH
♒	AQUARIUS	+	FIXED	AIR
♓	PISCES	−	MUTABLE	WATER

This table shows a summary of each sign's duality, quality and element. When you investigate a chart, you sum up the number of planets in each duality, quality and element, to obtain three different summaries: one for distribution of positive and negative planets, one for the qualities and one for the elements. On the data card for our sample chart on page 94, you'll find three positive and seven negative planets. It has three cardinal planets, five fixed and two mutable ones. One planet is in the element of fire, three are in earth, two in air and four in water. We can thus conclude that the planetary energies manifest themselves with a surplus of negative planets, a surplus of the fixed quality and of the water element, while the chart shows a deficit of the mutable quality and of the elements of fire and air.

Too much earth makes a person materialistic, unimaginative, cynical and narrow-minded.

Too much air makes a person overly theoretical, superficial, disorganized, indecisive and unable to act.

Too much water makes a person over-sensitive, anxious, gullible and self-repressive – the victim of his own exaggerated emotions.

It can be equally difficult to have a deficit of one element:

People with *insufficient fire* have a low energy level. They are fearful and insecure, often tense and suffering from the cold.

People with *insufficient earth* shun responsibilities and trivialities. They find it hard to accept material demands made on them and neglect their physical welfare.

People with *insufficient air* lack a perspective on themselves. They find it hard to co-operate and see other people's view. They are easily harassed.

People with *insufficient water* deny the importance of feelings – those of other people as well as their own. The result is emotional isolation.

6 The birth-chart

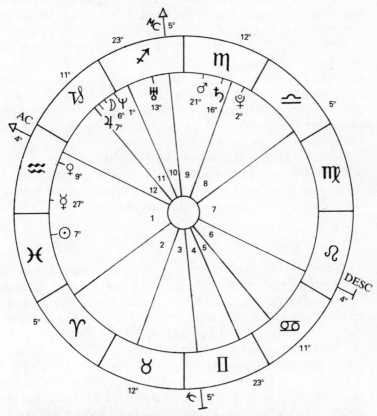

This is what a completed birth-chart looks like. It has been drawn up for a person born in London (00°06′W, 51°32′N) on 26 February 1984 at 05.50 a.m. (GMT) and will be used as a sample chart for reference throughout the book. For simplicity we use only whole degrees in charts.

If you draw a projection of the sky as it appeared from Earth at the moment of your birth – that is, a circle with the Earth at the centre – divided into twelve equal sectors, you have an astrological map: the beginning of your *birth-chart* or your *natal chart*.

The natal chart can be adjusted to both the place of birth and the minute you were born. It is therefore unique to each individual. It has not happened yet that two people were born simultaneously in the same place. Even one-egg twins are, for natural reasons, separated by an interval. The significance of that interval varies from case to case, but it can never be ignored.

As has already been mentioned, the eight planets, plus the Sun and Moon, all occupied different positions in the sky at your time of birth, scattered throughout the twelve Zodiacal signs. On the natal chart each body is inserted in its appropriate place, showing its position at that moment. (The planetary positions are given by computer or in astrological tables.)

Because it is a document depicting the sky at a given moment (the moment of birth), the natal chart never changes. What you can read out of it is your character, your motivations and, perhaps most of all, your potential.

The Ascendant

The birth-chart has as its starting-point the sign that rose on the eastern horizon at birth, as seen from the place of birth. This is called the *Ascendant*, or the *rising sign*. After it follow, counter-clockwise, the other eleven signs, in the sequence they have in the natural Zodiac (p. 44).

The eastern horizon, or the Ascendant, takes twenty-three hours and fifty-six minutes to complete the Zodiac, the time it takes the Earth to revolve once (360°) round its own axis. This is called sidereal time (star-time) and is used for calculating a chart. The Earth needs another four minutes to return to the same point in relation to the Sun, which moves one degree over the firmament in twenty-four hours (apparent motion of course, since it is the Earth that moves).

In order to find the exact position of the Ascendant, you have to take into account not only the minute of birth but also the longitude and latitude of the place of birth, as well as the inclination of the Earth's axis, Greenwich-time, sidereal time etc. Fortunately, these long calculations can now be done by computer, which also reduces the margin of error.

Since there are twelve signs in the Zodiac, the Ascendant spends an average of two hours in each. Due to the inclined axis of the Earth, the rhythm of the Ascendant becomes increasingly irregular the further north or south you go; only on the Equator is it quite even.

If it takes the Ascendant two hours to move through one sign – that is thirty degrees of the celestial Equator ($\frac{1}{12}$ of $360°=30°$) – it follows that it moves one degree in about four minutes. To make a chart specific, it is therefore necessary to assess not only the *sign* of the Zodiac rising on the horizon at the time of birth, seen from the place of birth, but also what *degree* of that sign.

There has been some discussion about the exact moment of birth. How and when should it be established? I agree with those who equal the beginning of human life to the moment when the baby passes from one element into another: when it leaves the liquid-surrounded existence in its mother's womb and for the first time relies on the air to feed it. The first breath must be regarded as the first token of independent life.This also answers any questions about induced births.

You may ask what happens if you don't know what time you were born. In that case you ought to try to estimate the most likely time – was it night, morning, afternoon? – and use that, but with a wide margin for the interpretation. You can also disregard the time factor completely and set up a chart for your *day of birth* instead. Such a chart has the Sun's position that day as its starting-point and is therefore called a solar chart. The solar chart is, of course, not unique like a natal chart, but it still contains a lot of important astrological information.

What the Ascendant stands for

The sign rising on the eastern horizon when you were born is an indication of the impression you give other people: your appearance as well as your spontaneous behaviour. The Ascendant is also connected with your early childhood, when patterns of behaviour were established without the influence of your inner will. The conflict between behaviour and intentions (Ascendant versus the Sun) explains why we're sometimes misunderstood and sometimes confused by our own actions. The Ascendant also gives an indication of the kind of experience we actively seek. It gears us towards the future and the fulfilment of our destiny.

The characteristics of the Ascendant sign are similar to those of the Sun sign, and both should be considered when a chart is interpreted. But remember that their functions differ. (See the description of the Sun on page 37.)

Since the Sun always rises in the sign it is presently occupying, people born at sunrise have their Ascendant in the same sign as the Sun. They are called 'double signs' and are particularly strong representatives of their Sun sign.

The Ascendant's ruler

An important factor in your natal chart is the planet ruling the sign occupied by your Ascendant. (See rulers, p. 46.) This is called the *Ascendant's ruler* and is likely to hold some special significance in the interpretation of your chart.

The Midheaven and the other angles

The Midheaven or, in Latin Medium Coeli, abbreviated MC, is the highest point in the sky (zenith) at the moment of birth.

The sign of the Midheaven and, perhaps even more, the planet ruling this sign (see rulers, p. 46) give you an idea of your vocational leanings and your own attitude to your career. The Midheaven also shows the social position you aspire to and your reputation. When the Midheaven is activated by stellar influences, you can expect dynamic happenings in your working or public life.

The Midheaven becomes particularly interesting if you find that you have a planet situated somewhere near it or right opposite it – that is, 180° away from it. It has been established that extremely successful people always have planets near the Midheaven or the Ascendant, or in so called opposition to them.

The Ascendant and the Midheaven and their two opposite points (which are called the Descendant and *Imum Coeli*, IC) together form the four so-called *angles* of the natal chart.

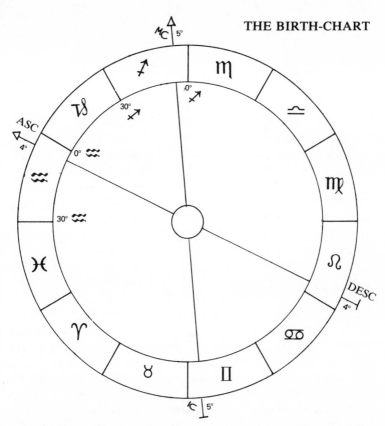

The beginning of a birth-chart with the Ascendant in Aquarius 4°24′ and the other three angles marked (see below).

Planets situated anywhere near these angles, in particular the ones near Ascendant or Midheaven, become strongly motivated. They generate huge amounts of energy and manifest themselves in a direct, inevitable manner.

A French statistician, Michel Gauquelin, decided a few years ago to test the traditional astrological claims with the aid of statistics and computers in a highly scientific context. One definite result of his investigation was the discovery that certain planets in *conjunction* with (immediate vicinity of) the Ascendant or Midheaven give a sharp increase or reduction (up to 25 per cent) of the frequency of different professional groups:

The Moon near the Ascendant or Midheaven was most common in authors and politicians.

61

Mars near the Ascendant or Midheaven was most common in executives, professional soldiers and athletes.

Jupiter near the Ascendant or Midheaven was most common in playwrights, journalists and ministers.

Saturn near the Ascendant or Midheaven was most common in doctors and scientists.

For his investigation, Gauquelin used an enormous sample: at least twenty thousand charts. This makes the statistical result very reliable. He was able to conduct his investigation in France because French authorities record the moment of birth on each birth certificate. Unfortunately, few countries have that practice, and the official documentation necessary for such investigations is lacking in most places.

The Nodes

The so-called nodes are the two points in your chart where the Moon crosses the ecliptic (the Equator). They have a certain significance, though nowhere near as great as that of the planets. The sign and house where the north node (Ω) is found indicate the direction your efforts should take for maximum benefit, while the south node ($\mho$) shows how you should tackle past experience for a minimum of restriction. The interpretation of the nodes becomes more relevant in advanced astrology, but they are not important enough to be included in the basic interpretations listed in Part Two of this book. Their position and aspects are, however, given on the data card (page 94) for those who want to go on to more advanced astrological studies.

The astrological houses

The so-called *astrological houses* are an abstract astrological aid, helping us define the effect of the planets in each individual case. They are decisive for the interpretation of a birth-chart.

There are twelve houses, as many as there are signs, and there is a correlation between them and the Zodiac, although they must be kept strictly apart. The houses are based on a division of the sky into twelve sectors, based on the Earth's

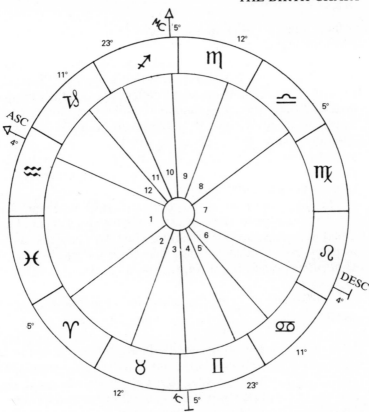

The beginning of a birth-chart with the Ascendant in Capricorn and Midheaven in Sagittarius. The twelve houses are also marked (see below).

rotation and the four angles of the chart. The starting-point is always the Ascendant.

For people born near the Equator, all houses are equally large, but their size varies increasingly the closer to the poles you get.

The houses are a relatively 'new' astrological invention – first used by the Greeks about 2,500 years ago. There are many different methods of calculating the houses – about ten house systems can be said to be useful in interpretation. All systems use the Ascendant and its opposite point, the Descendant, as their fixed points, but the other house *cusps* can be estimated in different ways.

63

The most popular house system in use today is that of Placidus, developed in the seventeenth century by an Italian monk and mathematician, Placidus de Tito. In 1821 a young astrologer called R.C. Smith, better known as 'Raphael', published an almanac including tables based on the Placidian house system. For a long time these tables were the only ones available in print, and they therefore became very widespread. Today, however, there are better, more accurate systems, such as Koch, the topocentric system and Campanus. In this book we shall use the topocentric system (see suggested reading p. 240).

The function of the houses is directly related to your daily life. In a horoscope, the houses tell us which *area* of your life is affected by a certain constellation. They show how the characteristics expressed by planets and signs are given *practical application*. Each house represents a specific sphere of *life experience*.

In personal astrology, the houses have the following significance:

HOUSE I	always starts with the Ascendant. It represents the face you show the world, your spontaneous self, your ego, your behaviour, your appearance and your self-assertion. Cf. Aries.
HOUSE II	represents material assets, such as income and possessions, but also your attitude to these things, and your principles in general. Cf. Taurus.
HOUSE III	stands for intellect, nerves, communication, verbal ability, shorter trips, neighbours, brothers and sisters and basic education. Cf. Gemini.
HOUSE IV	stands for the home, for security and your need of it. It also symbolizes your background, inherited characteristics and the beginning and end of your life. Cf. Cancer.
HOUSE V	represents creativity and self-projection and rules channels for this sort of thing: love, children and pleasure. It is also the house of speculation and gambling. Cf. Leo.

HOUSE VI   stands for work, service, duty and health and shows your experience of these things. It also symbolizes your limitations and self-criticism. Cf. Virgo.

HOUSE VII   represents partnerships – personal, marital or professional, and your attitude to close relationships. It also rules popularity and social life. Cf. Libra.

HOUSE VIII   stands for joint finances, our share in other people's money. It rules things like taxes, shares, insurance, inheritance, death and sexuality – and your way of handling these. Cf. Scorpio.

HOUSE IX   symbolizes knowledge, philosophy, religion, wisdom, higher education, foreign countries and languages. Your morals and conscience are also ruled by this house. Cf. Sagittarius.

HOUSE X   stands for your station in life, professional status, responsibilities and success. Your effect on – and attitude to – authorities and the established society. Cf. Capricorn.

HOUSE XI   represents friends, societies, organizations and ideologies. Purpose in life and objectives, on an intellectual or spiritual level. Cf. Aquarius.

HOUSE XII   symbolizes the subconscious, future plans, secrets, inspiration, hidden talents, restrictions, disappointments, escapism, self-destruction and institutions. Cf. Pisces.

7 Aspects

A considerable extra dimension is added to the interpretation of a chart by the so-called *aspects*. These provide a profound and subtle insight into a person's character. An aspect can be regarded as a charge or discharge of energy; it describes the person's inner dynamics and points out the channels available for their release.

The aspects are found by measuring *the angle between two*

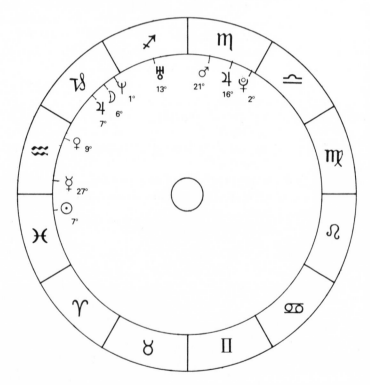

The sample chart with all planets in their exact position. For clarity, houses, Ascendant and Midheaven are not marked.

planets in the birth-chart. (To make things easier, we are now talking of the Sun and Moon as planets, too, although this is not technically correct.) To be able to do this accurately, you must take into account the exact position of each planet – that is, assess what degree of the sign it occupies, counting counter-clockwise from the beginning of the sign. The calculation of the aspects can be done manually, but this is a long time-consuming exercise which is now unnecessary, as a computer easily provides all aspects. On the other hand, you ought to know how the angles are found.

You start with each planet's position in the birth-chart, its sign and degree:

When the angle between two planets is measured, the Earth is used as the point of intersection (see Figures on p. 68–69). If this angle amounts to a certain even number of degrees, the planets are said to form an *aspect* between them. Each planetary aspect has its own special significance, depending on i) the aspect itself, ii) the planets it involves, iii) their respective signs and iv) the houses these planets occupy.

The angles counting as *major aspects* are: 0°, 60° 90°, 120°, 180°. There are also some minor aspects (30°, 45°, 135°, 150°) but in this book we shall concentrate on the more important, major ones.

The aspects, just like planets and signs, are marked by symbols:

0°: The aspect is called a *conjunction* and is marked by ☌.
60°: The aspect is called a *sextile* and is marked by ✶.
90°: The aspect is called a *square* and is marked by □.
120°: The aspect is called a *trine* and is marked by △.
180°: The aspect is called an *opposition* and is marked by ☍.

Aspect deviation – orb

It's very unusual that two planets measure an exact number of degrees such as 0°, 60° etc. It has been established that the aspect works even if there is a small deviation. The margin allowed for interpretation is called *the orb*. The orb varies for different aspects and planets. Generally, it can be said that the greater the orb, the weaker the aspect. The table below shows the orb recommended in this book – its exact size has always

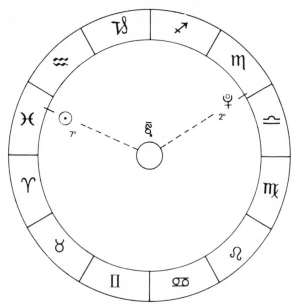

This is two of the planets in the sample chart on page 57. The Sun in Pisces 7° and Pluto in Scorpio 2° are within the permitted orb for the trine aspect (120°, orb 9°). Interpretation p. 173.

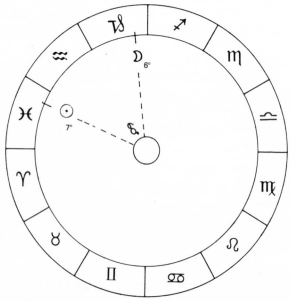

The Moon in Capricorn 6° sextile. The Sun in Pisces 7°. Interpretation p. 169.

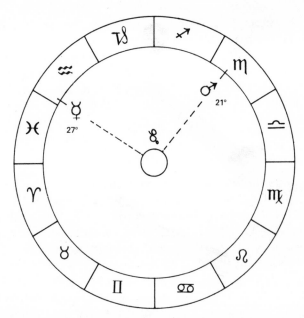

In this instance, Mercury in Aquarius 27° is square. Mars in Scorpio 21° with an orb of 7°, which means that the aspect is relatively weak. Interpretation p. 178.

been a bone of contention amongst astrologers. We allow a slightly larger orb for aspects involving the Sun or Moon, due to their stronger influence.

Aspect		Orb	Sun/Moon
☌	0°	7°	9°
✷	60°	5°	7°
☐	90°	7°	9°
△	120°	7°	9°
☍	180°	7°	9°

Soft and hard aspects

Experience has shown that the effect of an aspect can be either *soft* (harmonious) or *hard* (discordant). In traditional astrology, these were sometimes termed 'good' and 'bad', but that kind of judgement is highly subjective and not recommended. Ancient astrology, incidentally, had an attitude to the aspects which differed greatly from that of European astrologers, because their moral and philosophical outlook was so different. One way to avoid evaluations is to call the aspects soft and hard. They are, in fact, not at all objective, but indicate a person's own attitude to different sides of his character.

Characteristics of the aspects

☌ *0°, the conjunction:* When two planets in a chart are in exactly the same position – that is, when the angle between them is 0° – they are said to be in conjunction. This is the most powerful of all aspects. It affects character as well as circumstances, concentrates power and accumulates energy. Under favourable conditions, this energy flows freely, but when they are less favourable, the energy may be blocked, and the conjunction becomes more like a square or opposition (see below). The conjunction is either soft (☌S), neutral (☌N) or hard (☌H), depending on the planets involved and other aspects to the conjunction. In Part Two on p. 167 there is a diagram showing how the different conjunctions are to be interpreted. Also, each aspect interpretation (pp. 169–189) is marked by ☌S, ☌N or ☌H, to show how a conjunction should be read.

⚹ *60°, the sextile:* This aspect appears when the angle between two planets amounts to 60°. It's a soft aspect, mainly affecting your mental faculties. It shows that the two planets complement each other, strengthening and improving each other, so that ideas, contacts and opportunities flow freely and easily, sometimes to the extent that the person takes them for granted. But even if these abstract advantages do not manifest themselves in a very conspicuous manner, they are a good asset to have in a chart. The sextile opens up your mind to new impressions and gives you an independent spirit.

□ *90°, the square:* When two planets are at a right angle to each other (90° apart), they are said to form a square. This is a hard aspect, indicating that the two planets involved are in direct conflict with each other. The square checks the fulfilment of ambitions and aspirations, blocks energy and creates tension. On the other hand, this blocked energy craves a release, and the aspect therefore often assumes the function of a prime mover. If the person affected by it can learn to live with the conflict, not rejecting one planet in favour of another, the result is usually great achievements.

△ *120°, the trine:* This aspect, formed by two planets with 120° between them, is the softest of all aspects. It breeds harmony and is creative and favourable, active and idealistic. You couldn't ask for a more constructive element in a chart, because the two planets involved co-operate happily for the same purpose, supporting and bringing out the very best in each other. The trine is also an indication of talent in one field or an other – but the urge or the motivation to develop it is not always present.

♂ *180°, the opposition:* This aspect, which indicates that two planets are placed exactly opposite each other in a chart, is a hard aspect, mainly concerned with relationships. It will challenge the person affected by it, inducing him to see other people's point of view and forcing on him compromise and co-operation. The opposition also represents the influence of other people. Moreover, it enables the person to see two different sides of his own needs, as reflected by the two conflicting planets involved. This insight can be used constructively and help avoid the danger of letting the planets enter a tug-of-war. The opposition, like the square, shows the areas in life where a person has to struggle most, but also where he has the greatest chance to develop and achieve good results.

The T-square, the Grand Cross and the Grand Trine

When two planets in a chart together from an opposition, and there is a third planet making square aspects to each of them, you have what is called a *T-square*. This conglomeration of hard aspects can certainly be a cross to bear, but it is nevertheless found in the charts of many tremendously successful people.

The *Grand Cross*, involving four planets which are all in

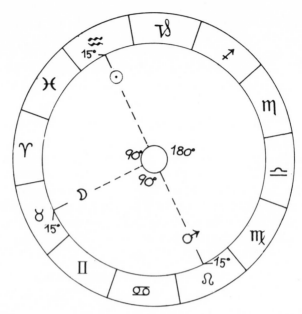

T-square.

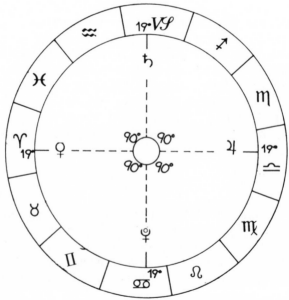

Grand Cross.

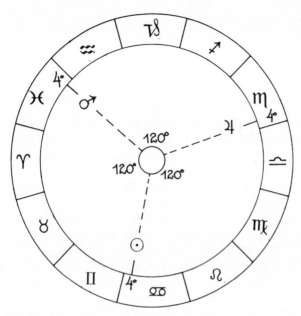

Grand Trine.

Since these aspects are not present in our sample chart, we show three theoretical constellations.

opposition and square to each other, is an unusual but extremely powerful feature to have in a chart. It needs to be studied carefully for soft points of balance which can act as channels for its dammed-up energy.

The *Grand Trine*, on the other hand, consists of three planets which are all in trine to each other. This is a fantastic asset to have – provided it is properly exploited. Much too often it remains dormant, like so many other soft aspects, under a cover of complacency, self-sufficiency and a lack of motivation.

Soft and hard placing

If a planet in a chart receives several soft aspects, that planet is said to be *softly placed*. It means that all the best sides of the planet and its sign flourish and that there is a very good potential to realize.

If a planet in a chart receives several hard aspects, that planet is said to be *hard placed*. Then the planet's and the sign's more destructive features threaten to take over, and conscious control is necessary to overcome them.

The balance

Because the function of the soft aspects is to *mould* the potential, whereas the task of the hard aspects is to *release* it, it is logical that an ideal chart should have an even distribution of the two. Some horoscopes, however, have a marked imbalance in either direction, although it's rare to find a chart with exclusively soft or hard aspects.

People with pronounced soft charts tend to be idle and spoilt by life. As a consequence they become demanding; their character is weak and their resistance low. In extreme cases they are prone to alcoholism, drug abuse or uncalled-for nervous breakdowns. If the person himself is wise enough to direct his favourable conditions out, away from himself, he becomes both healthier and happier. Pronounced soft charts have a tendency to attract those worse off, and such people often find that they take on other people's problems. Soft aspects are not a personal asset to indulge in but a gift to be shared, a responsibility, and they become useful only when properly applied.

A multitude of *hard* aspects show what we have to struggle against but also where our energy is extracted. They always indicate a certain amount of tension, inner conflict, blockages, obstacles and hard work, but at the same time they hold a promise of strength and dynamic personal development. And even if one doesn't like to see anyone born with the *Grand Cross* hanging round his neck, it is inevitable that *hard* aspects urge people to achieve outstanding feats. The *fixed T-square* (involving planets in *fixed* signs) can move mountains, provided the owner manages to co-ordinate his own conflicting traits. The *cardinal T-square* (involving planets in *cardinal* signs) is a tremendous generator of power but can be dangerous if the masses of energy are misdirected. A *mutable T-square* (involving planets in *mutable* signs) can be the very incitement needed by this person, but the tendency to become nervous, distraught, dejected and disappointed must be actively fought.

Wherever there are strong *hard* aspects, the chart should be examined for *soft* points of balance that can mitigate the destructive potential and encourage the positive manifestation of the planets involved.

Strong and weak placing

There is also the concept of *strongly or weakly placed* planets in a natal chart. A strongly placed planet is one receiving several major aspects. Such a planet acquires the function of an anchor for the character and becomes a source of strength and security.

A weakly placed planet is one that receives minor or no aspects. Such a planet can be more of a problem than one that is hard placed, because it represents a side of the personality which is unintegrated, lacking in function, in limbo, as it were, without an outlet for its inherent power. People with relatively few aspects in their chart are often confused and unmotivated: they tend to drift with no definite purpose in life. If you are one of those, you must make sure to take advantage of any transitory activation of your chart (see the next chapter on predictive astrology).

Normally, each planet in a chart has one or two, often more, major aspects, averaging a total of at least twenty aspects in a chart.

8 Predictive astrology

The ancient Greeks used to say that no man can swim in the same river twice – because everything flows. In the same way life flows: we develop and change a little every minute of the day, as our life experience mounts up. You are now a slightly different person from the one you were when you woke up this morning.

Some philosophical theories maintain that the sole purpose of our existence here on earth is to increase our experience – that is, to develop, or change. Astrology subscribes to that idea. It shows that life is one long process of changing circumstances. The best we can do is to go along with the changes imposed on us by fluctuating conditions. Fighting or resisting them can be dangerous, because it blocks energy and can lead to a more drastic alteration of our situation. On the other hand, by understanding the need for and the nature of these changes, we can learn to control them and ensure that they serve rather than thwart our purposes. The threat to our *status quo* is the first step towards improving it.

The world horoscope

A horoscope for any given moment reveals not only the character of an individual born at that time but also the face of the world as it appeared then. Just like any birth-chart, the *world horoscope* is a time-related map of the firmament, taking into account the position of each planet in our solar system, plus the Sun and Moon.

As you know, some of the heavenly bodies move very fast, whereas others remain in the same sign for years, even decades. This means that the world horoscope shows a very complex picture: on the one hand, superficial influences that change overnight; on the other, major social processes which take many years to mature.

The world chart tells us what is going on in the world at that moment. When there is strife and conflict in the world horoscope, wars and disasters take place, while peace and relative opulence prevail when the chart is harmonious and expansive. Where in the world different events manifest themselves depends on the so called geographical astrology. Each country is supposed to be ruled by a certain traditionallly established starsign.

An interesting example is the Falkland crisis of 1982. At the time of the Argentinian invasion, there was a powerful opposition in the sky between the Sun in Aries and Mars in Libra. You may remember that Aries is the sign traditionally ruled by Mars, the planet of war and strife, and that the opposition is a symbol of conflicting relations. Add to that the fact that Britain is traditionally ruled by Aries and Argentina by Libra, and you'll have an idea of the secrets contained by the world chart. It is also fascinating to note the attitude of each side to the conflict: the Argentinians defended their actions with something they called justice (Libra), whereas the Britons relied more on principles and military force (Aries).

The world chart also explains why many of us – not only wine connoisseurs – often agree that certain years are better or worse than others, on a socio-political as well as on a personal level.

Due to the planetary motion, the world horoscope is constantly changing. Only a minute after your birth, the world picture and the internal relations of the Universe had changed slightly. The world chart as it appears today will naturally be very different from your birth-chart. If you take the world chart for today (or any other day in the past, present or future) and compare it to your own birth-chart, you can learn to tell from the relations between the world planets and your own natal planets how the universal picture at a particular moment affects you personally. This is the basis of all personal predictive astrology.

Another, simpler method is to compare the world chart with each one of the twelve Sunsigns and see how it relates to each one. This is what newspaper astrologers do. By now you probably realize why such forecasts are very generalized: they

77

take into account only the position of your Sun and disregard the rest of your natal chart. Daily forecasts are based mainly on the movement of the Moon, the fastest-moving body, whose influence passes rapidly, without much significance to the life of the person concerned.

In predictive astrology, it's the slow-moving planets that are the most interesting. Jupiter, for example, spends one year in each sign. In other words, the planet occupies your Sunsign once every twelve years. (see Figure on p. 34). This should be a successful, flourishing period in your life (see also pp. 38–41). Saturn settles in your Sunsign for 2½ years, at intervals of about 29½ years. That is usually experienced as a trying period.

Only some of us are in for a direct encounter with Uranus, Neptune or Pluto in our lifetime, because they spend many years in each sign. These very slow-moving planets represent long-lasting and profound personal and social transformation. Many people find it difficult to put a finger on their influence while it lasts, but it's usually obvious in hindsight. Because of their deep and strong influence on the individual, even their rhythm is noticeable: Uranus's cycle of seven years in each sign or house and Neptune's of about fourteen years normally coincide with important stages of inner – and outer – development. The same goes for Pluto, whose cycle varies between fifteen and thirty-five years in each sign.

Transits

When a planet in the world chart at a given moment assumes a position where it forms a *major aspect* to a planet in your natal chart, this is said to be a *transit*. By comparing the planets of the world chart with those in your birth-chart, you can assess whether any of the world planets are forming transits to your natal planets. The method is the same as that used for finding the natal *aspects*: you measure the angle between each transiting planet and each planet of your natal chart, using the Earth as the point of intersection.

When a planet in the world chart makes a transit – that is, forms a major aspect to a planet in your natal chart – this will coincide with an important experience in your life. It may

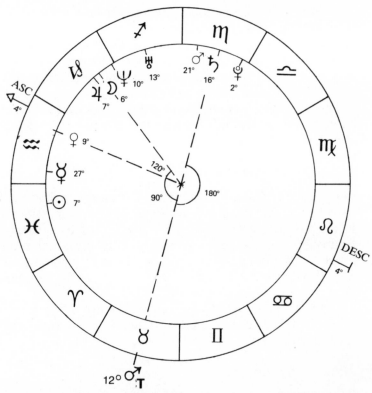

On a day when Mars was in a position of 12° in Taurus, the planet formed the above transit aspects to our sample chart. Using the same orb as for natal aspects (page 69), we can conclude that Mars in transit on the day in question formed an opposition to the sample chart's natal Saturn, a trine to the natal Moon and Jupiter, a square to the natal Venus and a sextile to the natal Sun. In the same way, the transiting aspects of each other planet can be assessed for interpretation (pp. 191–213).

manifest itself as an external event but could just as well be an important phase of inner development. Its effect often goes out from within, whether or not you're aware of it: the attitude you develop under a transit causes the kind of event which is its external manifestation. When was the last time something dramatic happened in your life? Try to reconstruct your feelings leading up to that incident, and you may understand what I mean.

In Part Two of this book, the Transit interpretation (pp. 191–213) describes the transits of Mars, Jupiter, Saturn, Uranus, Neptune and Pluto to each of the natal planets. These six are the planets that lie beyond Earth in the solar system, and they represent the more significant changes in our lives. Their transits can go on for years.

The inner planets also form regular transits to the natal chart, but these last only for a short time and rarely affect life as a whole.

Solar and lunar returns

One method regularly to assess one's transits is to draw up the world chart for the day of the Sun's annual return (the solar return) to the exact position it occupies in your birth-chart (on or around your birthday). During your solar year, all planets move to different positions, and the places they occupy on the day of your solar return give you the forecast for the coming year.

In the same way, the Moon's (lunar) return to its position in your birth-chart can be used each month as the basis of your monthly forecast.

How to interpret a transit

Some astrologers differentiate between *soft* and *hard* transits, just like aspects. In this book both sides of a transit are described in the transit interpretation in Part Two, but the effect of a transit has much to do with your own mental outlook.

It is by all means pleasant when a benevolent planet (like Jupiter) in the world chart forms a soft aspect in transit to an equally benevolent softly placed (p. 73) planet in your birth-chart. It makes you so positive and generous that other people bend over backwards in order to please you. Everything you touch brings luck, success breeds success and life couldn't be nicer – pity it's only for a limited period, as long as the transit lasts.

In the same way, it is indeed tiresome to have a dynamic planet (like Mars) forming a hard aspect in transit to another strong, hard-placed planet (p. 73) in one's natal chart. If the trouble doesn't come first, we develop a mood so nasty that it actually provokes others to sabotage all our efforts and make our temper even worse. The vicious circle may be there for as long as the transit lasts – fortunately not for ever.

But the function of transits is not as simple as that. If every soft transit were to let the manna rain over you, while you sat yourself down comfortably to just enjoy it, the result would be a stunning fear of any hard transit, which would then deal one blow after another to perfectly innocent people, at it's own arbitrary discretion.

As it turns out, life is fairer than that. To a very large extent we can decide for ourselves what our life is to be. To enjoy a fruit, you first have to plant a tree. Happiness and success seldom come for nothing – and if they do, you can rest assured that the bill will be presented after delivery of the goods. Everything has a price.

A soft transit simply offers favourable circumstances and good opportunities to sow what will be reaped at a later date, and to reap that which has already been sown.

A hard transit, on the other hand, will challenge us and make demands. It forces us to take the consequences of our previous actions. One possible effect of a hard transit is the exposure of cheating and neglect. If you're one of these who set traps for others, you may find that you've been caught in one yourself. Hard transits ensure that we build life on honest and safe foundations and may indicate that we're on the wrong track.

Sometimes a person goes through a prolonged period of calamity. On the face of it, his various misfortunes may seem totally unrelated. But if you look into the problems deeply enough, you will find that they all emanate from the same basic misdirection: they are all different expressions of one developing process and all contain the same message. As soon as the person realizes what life is trying to tell him, he can start using the circumstances and learn to take advantage of even the hardest transit. It will then manifest itself more like the soft side of the same transit.

A transit should never be seen as an isolated incident. It's a link in a chain of events leading up to it and continuing after it's over. The whole process is best understood by preceding and following transits, which join forces to effectuate some necessary change in your life. If you oppose that change, it is possible that something will 'happen' to force it on you. But if you accept that it is inevitable and, in the long run, leading to something better, you'll find the experience more interesting than traumatic.

On the other hand, it would be hypocrisy to suggest that all transits can be lived through without pain. To most people, nothing is more frightening than a shattering of the *status quo*, on which they have based their whole existence. Even so, seen in its right context, perhaps years after it happened, each transit can be explained and understood. And then it usually turns out that, of the things that happen to us in life, it's very few that don't carry within them the seed of something good.

Worrying about approaching transits is totally fruitless. And do not use them in an attempt to predict future events – they appear in thousands of different guises and you're unlikely to make an appropriate guess. What you can do, however, is to use a reverse method: if your life shows a pattern of regularly occurring problems, you can investigate the ephemeris to assess what regular transits provoke these. That will give you a chance of both tracing the source of your problems and preparing yourself, mentally and physically, for the next demanding period. Forewarned is forearmed. Healthy living, rest and exercise in a sound balance always help before a battle. And although you can't establish what is to happen under the transit, you can predict *trends* and reflect on their nature.

If you suddenly find yourself in the middle of a difficult transit – that is, a crisis – there is only one antidote: study the transit and try to understand it. Each transit presents an opportunity to overcome innate weaknesses and conflicts. If you merely choose to count the days until the transit is over, the problem will be there again to cause another crisis at the next transit. What you should do is seize the opportunity to settle it once and for all.

Progressions

Another factor used by advanced astrologers in predictive

astrology is *progressions*. If you consult a professional astrologer, it may help to know that these are an extension of your natal chart, showing the course of your inner personal development, without relating it to external influences like the transits.

The principle behind progressions is the idea of a progressive unfolding of every aspect of nature, including our own personality.

You may find, when you come to interpret your birth-chart, that the potential expressed by it has been more or less noticeable during different phases of your life. This is due to the fluctuation of progressions. Generally one could say that *progressions emphasize characteristics and bring out your potential. Transits*, on the other hand, *provoke experiences.* You can imagine the dynamic effect when some point in your natal chart is activated simultaneously by both progressions and transits. The houses and the planets and signs involved in this massive stimulation will give you an idea of its manifestation.

There are several different, abstract mathematical methods to trace progressions in a chart. Just like transits, progressions are found by measuring the angle between progressed planets and natal planets. Only the progressions of the Sun, Moon, Venus, Mars and Mercury are significant. If one of these forms an exact aspect, particularly a *conjunction*, to a planet in your natal chart, the sphere of life indicated by the house, planet and sign will be strongly activated. If this conjunction is also stimulated by a *transit* from the world chart, you have definitely reached a milestone in your life.

The dramatic *events* that normally ensue are mostly determined by the transit affecting the natal planet and the progression. The *outcome* on the other hand, the long-term effect, depends on the natal chart. I've seen a case where a person won the pools on such an occasion but lost all the money due to bad management, and another who was almost killed in an accident but saved by an unbelievable stroke of luck. The first natal chart showed bad financial judgement and the other longevity.

So even when it comes to predictive astrology, the first thing is to understand and come to terms with your own natal chart, on which everything else rests.

It is useful to know that horoscopes are affected by progressions, but they do belong to an advanced method of interpretation which is beyond the scope of this book, and if you wish to learn more about them, specific astrological studies will be necessary.

9   Synastry

Synastry, comparative astrology, means that you analyse the aspects formed between the planets of two different birth-charts and then interpret them to get an idea of the relationship between the two people involved. It can be applied to any kind of human relations, from distant to close, from love or family to business or work, to people of the same or the opposite sex, to people of the same age or different generations. Because synastry informs us about things which we don't always see clearly, it's particularly valid where close emotional ties are concerned.

Synastry is an essential part of astrological study. The main objective is of course to increase one's self-knowledge – but what good is that if it doesn't lead to any improvement in your relations with other people? No one exists alone.

To suggest that there is such as a thing as a perfect relationship or an ideal partner would be an exaggeration. There is always an element of conflict, although we may choose different ways of dealing with it. On the other hand, there are cases where two people spend most of their lives together in comparative harmony, where they grow and flourish together, well aware that they would never have been able to realize their full potential without the help of the partner. Likewise, there are plenty of relationships based on mutual destruction and controversy. And the worst thing about destructive combinations is their tendency to survive, even if the souls of the couple don't. Nothing ties people together like conflict and power struggle.

Most relationships, however, are less extreme. Usually they are a mixture of good and bad; the more harmonious points make up for those less harmonious. Identifying the strengths and weaknesses of a particular combination can be very useful, as well as finding out what good or bad character-istics the relationship brings out in each person. This can all be done with synastry.

If two people together can put the finger on potential or acute conflicts, if they can agree to differ on certain incompatible points, they can also work out a compromise acceptable to both of them. Those who have spent a lifetime together have probably learnt to do this already – or they wouldn't still be together – but at the beginning of a shared life it is very important that you learn to avoid the pitfalls, to stop them eroding the relationship and undermining its best possibilities.

In case you're hesitant whether or not to commit yourself to another person, synastry can tell you exactly what makes you hesitate. It won't make the decision for you but works rather like consumer information: specifying the quality of the goods, giving directions for use and not least, indicating the price you have to pay for it. Moreover, it gives practical hints on how to handle it for best results.

You can also estimate your *synastric transits* and the timing of possible future crises. If you can assess the duration and severity of an oncoming crisis, you won't be caught by a sudden breakdown of communication between you. If you understand what is happening and why, you can fight back, perhaps even avert it. Preferably this should be done by a joint effort.

Synastric aspects are easier to interpret than personal ones, because they are closer to the surface, and not subject to the same kind of psychological processing and repression as the personal aspects. More than anything, they reveal the *motives* for each particular combination.

For example, when one person's hard planets (Mars, Saturn, Uranus and, above all, Pluto) make hard aspects to the partner's planets, you usually have a person with low self-esteem who is covering up by using the partner as a screen, onto which he can project his identity. The partner is suppressed and rarely given a chance to develop – indeed, any attempt at independence on the side of the partner is seen as a serious threat to the already feeble ego and therefore vehemently opposed. This type of combination has good chances of surviving: the suppressed partner will soon be totally dependent and certainly has a nice comfortable life without any responsibility for his/her own person – but look at the cost of it!

A comparable type of relationship is that when the soft planets (Sun, Moon, Venus, Jupiter and Neptune) in each chart form hard aspects to those of the other person. Then both use each other for their personal gratification, often as a shortcut to a false identity. The relationship lasts for as long as both parties can stand living in a charade.

The prospects for happiness and harmony are better if the combination is based on identification through similarity – that is, where the same sign, element or duality (pp. 46–55) are represented – the two people may have the same Sunsign or year of birth. Each of them has then taken up with his own reflection and they share everything: background, interests, ambitions, hobbies, values etc. To begin with, these combinations are a source of great security and satisfaction, warding off the terror of loneliness. But sooner or later the total togetherness will prove limiting. Everyone requires a certain amount of breathing-space and self-realization, and that experience – sadly – cannot be shared. For a relationship like this to survive, it is vital that both parties accept and encourage each other's uniqueness rather than deny it.

Then there is the kind of combination where two people complement each other by adding something that the other one lacks, such as a missing quality or element (pp. 49–55). This can bring problems over identification – both parties must make a determined effort to understand and respect even that which is completely alien to them and trust each other, even when their modes of expression are entirely opposite. Still, relationships like these are often very strong, and the mutual sympathy is of a higher order. They also call for intense personal development, as this is the only way out of the inevitable conflicts. For people who dare, it's an exciting choice. But with all the differences, there is a constant threat of discord.

Modern people seem to be preoccupied with close relations – more than ever before. It is quite a good thing that we've come to expect more of each other. The high divorce rate and all the broken homes are probably a transitory stage of social development due to the fact that we are changing the foundations of personal relationships. No more do we have to marry people because of social pressures or dependence, but

87

we can choose our partner from a deeply personal point of view. We are more and more marrying for love, not to cover up unwanted pregnancies or to reap social or financial advantages. But in our search for genuine love and sympathy, we need more self-knowledge and discrimination than ever before. A lot of misery could be avoided if everyone knew exactly what he or she is expecting from a relationship – how much they are prepared to give and to what extent their expectations are realistic. Synastry will tell you how to assess just that.

10   If it doesn't make sense

If you find that the interpretation of your birth-chart doesn't make sense, there may be many reasons for this. First of all, interpretations in a book are never as exhaustive as a personal consultation with an astrologer – provided this is a professional, experienced person whose moral standards are up to his task. However, most erratic interpretations are due to the birth-time given incorrectly.

On the other hand, this is a good opportunity to scrutinize your own self-image. Is the interpretation really incorrect – or could it be that your idea of yourself is distorted, for better or for worse? Often things like excessive modesty, humility, eagerness to please, misdirected consideration, self-denial, wishful thinking, self-deception, self-discipline, self-repression, conceit, guilt, etc. keep us from seeing ourselves as we really are. Many people are unable to admit to having any faults at all, because they have been brought up to believe that they must be infallible.

Surely, it's understandable if you defend yourself against the insinuation that certain sides of your character are destructive and, to your own mind, unpleasant. It takes courage to accept them as being part of yourself. But as long as you deny their existence, you have no chance of getting the better of them. When a birth-chart is activated by progressions and transits, the person is usually given the opportunity to come to terms with negative character traits. Sooner or later you will find yourself in a confrontation where you have to decide whether or not to let them take over. If you pass the test, the destructive side of the trait will recede, and along with it will go a source of conflict and pain. Your life will suddenly take a turn for the better. On the other hand, if you take the line of least resistance and give in to destructive behaviour, it is likely to backfire on you: you'll be inviting destruction in your life. Make sure you're not in the risk zone.

Another explanation why it doesn't make sense may be that

your life hasn't quite started. Perhaps you have yet to experience one of those periods when self-realization is within reach? These periods can be trying, but they are also intensely satisfying, and it seems to be at these times that astrological interpretation is right on target. If you can look back on such a period in your past, you may have learnt already that which astrology sets out to teach: that circumstances can be controlled, that no one has to be victimized by them, that you can go beyond your limitations and explore areas you previously thought were beyond you.

Bear in mind that your horoscope is trying to tell you something. It's up to you to figure out what it is. Basically, it advises you to be honest with yourself and go along with your destiny. Your destiny is not your fate – it is your potential. If you oppose it, life may well use external measures to ensure that you develop into the person you're intended to be. Remember that it's not only your right but also your duty to be yourself. The world needs the person you really are – above all, it needs people who are real and genuine.

You need never fear the truth. When you see yourself in the large universal perspective with every piece of the jigsaw puzzle suddenly falling into place, when the image of your destiny emerges for the first time in all its perfection, then you've gained an insight which is well worth the risks and the effort. And you can continue on your way with full faith in life and no fear of the future.

PART TWO

Interpretation

1 Your data

Before you can start interpreting your birth-chart, you need a number of astrological data. If you send the information specified on p. 10 with your cheque to the address given, you will receive all the data you need to interpret and, if you like, draw up your chart on the form provided at the end of the book (p. 239). You can, however, go straight to the interpretations on pp. 125–237 to find those which apply to you. It will be as easy as using an encyclopaedia. You will also be able to establish your so-called potential with the questionnaire on pp. 100–107.

If you want to interpret more horoscopes or have a synastric analysis made, send the same information for the people concerned to the same address. Remember to write your own name and the address where you want the data sent. For each person, date, place and time of birth, as exact as possible, should be given.

Overleaf you will see the completed data card for our sample chart.

Some guidelines for interpreting the sample chart (p. 57)

The greatest difficulty when interpreting a chart is to synthesize a mass of astrological facts into a meaningful whole.

To lead us through the maze of astrological factors which all have a rôle to play, there is a simple, straightforward method. First of all, you examine the distribution of positive and negative signs, of qualities and elements (p. 46–56). Check the data card to see how many planets appear in each group. In the sample chart we have a preponderance of negative signs, no fewer than seven, against three positive. The dominating quality is the fixed one: three planets in Scorpio and two in Aquarius, five all told. Of the elements, water prevails: four

YOUR DATA

DATE OF BIRTH: 26.021984
PLACE OF BIRTH: LONDON
TIME OF BIRTH: 05.50

SIGNS AND HOUSE OF EACH PLANET

SUN	IS 06 DEGREES 50 MINUTES IN PISCES	IN HOUSE I
MERCURY	IS 27 DEGREES 24 MINUTES IN AQUARIUS	IN HOUSE I
VENUS	IS 08 DEGREES 42 MINUTES IN AQUARIUS	IN HOUSE I
MARS	IS 20 DEGREES 35 MINUTES IN SCORPIO	IN HOUSE IX
JUPITER	IS 07 DEGREES 15 MINUTES IN CAPRICORN	IN HOUSE XI
SATURN	IS 16 DEGREES 23 MINUTES IN SCORPIO	IN HOUSE IX
URANUS	IS 13 DEGREES 22 MINUTES IN SAGITTARIUS	IN HOUSE X
NEPTUNE	IS 01 DEGREES 04 MINUTES IN CAPRICORN	IN HOUSE XI
PLUTO	IS 01 DEGREES 60 MINUTES IN SCORPIO	IN HOUSE VIII
MOON	IS 06 DEGREES 10 MINUTES IN CAPRICORN	IN HOUSE XI
NODE	IS 11 DEGREES 33 MINUTES IN GEMINI	IN HOUSE IV

ASTROLOGICAL HOUSE CUSPS

THE TOPOCENTRIC HOUSE SYSTEM HAS BEEN USED IN THE CALCUATIONS
RULING PLANET IS URANUS

HOUSE I EQUALS THE ASCENDANT, HOUSE X EQUALS THE MIDHEAVEN

HOUSE I	IS 04 DEGREES 24 MINUTES IN AQUARIUS
HOUSE II	IS 04 DEGREES 35 MINUTES IN ARIES
HOUSE III	IS 11 DEGREES 44 MINUTES IN TAURUS
HOUSE X	IS 04 DEGREES 39 MINUTES IN SAGITTARIUS
HOUSE XI	IS 22 DEGREES 55 MINUTES IN SAGITTARIUS
HOUSE XII	IS 10 DEGREES 52 MINUTES IN CAPRICORN

POSITIVE AND NEGATIVE SIGNS

POSITIVE SIGNS:	MERCURY	VENUS	URANUS	NODE	
NEGATIVE SIGNS:	SUN	MARS	JUPITER	SATURN	NEPTUNE
	PLUTO			MOON	

PLANETS' DISTRIBUTION IN QUALITIES

CARDINAL SIGNS:	JUPITER	NEPTUNE	MOON		
FIXED SIGNS:	MERCURY	VENUS	MARS	SATURN	PLUTO
MUTABLE SIGNS:	SUN	URANUS	NODE		

PLANETS' DISTRIBUTION IN ELEMENTS

PLANETS IN FIRE:	URANUS			
PLANETS IN EARTH:	JUPITER	NEPTUNE	MOON	
PLANETS IN AIR:	MERCURY	VENUS	NODE	
PLANETS IN WATER:	SUN	MARS	SATURN	PLUTO

------MAJOR ASPECTS------

SUN	SEXTILE	MOON	SUN	SEXTILE	JUPITER
SUN	SQUARE	URANUS	SUN	SEXTILE	NEPTUNE
SUN	TRINE	PLUTO			
MOON	CONJUNCT	JUPITER	MOON	CONJUNCT	NEPTUNE
MOON	SEXTILE	PLUTO	MERCURY	SQUARE	MARS
MERCURY	SEXTILE	NEPTUNE	MERCURY	TRINE	PLUTO
VENUS	SQUARE	SATURN	VENUS	SEXTILE	URANUS
VENUS	SQUARE	PLUTO			
MARS	CONJUNCT	SATURN	JUPITER	CONJUNCT	NEPTUNE
JUPITER	SEXTILE	PLUTO	NEPTUNE	SEXTILE	PLUTO

------PRESENT TRANSITS------

THE PLANETS ARE CALCULATED FOR GMT AT NOON FOR DATE = 01.101984

MARS	= 27 DEGREES 26 MINUTES IN SAGITTARIUS
JUPITER	= 04 DEGREES 45 MINUTES IN CAPRICORN
SATURN	= 14 DEGREES 24 MINUTES IN SCORPIO
URANUS	= 10 DEGREES 22 MINUTES IN SAGITTARIUS
NEPTUNE	= 28 DEGREES 47 MINUTES IN SAGITTARIUS
PLUTO	= 01 DEGREES 09 MINUTES IN SCORPIO
NODE	= 29 DEGREES 60 MINUTES IN TAURUS

------TRANSITING PLANETS' ASPECTS TO NATAL HOROSCOPE------

FIRST TRANSITING PLANET, THEN THE ASPECT AND LAST THE PLANET IN THE NATAL HOROSCOPE THAT IS ASPECTED

MARS	SEXTILE	MERCURY	MARS	CONJUNCT	NEPTUNE
MARS	SEXTILE	PLUTO	JUPITER	SEXTILE	SUN
JUPITER	CONJUNCT	MOON	JUPITER	CONJUNCT	JUPITER
JUPITER	CONJUNCT	NEPTUNE	JUPITER	SEXTILE	PLUTO
SATURN	TRINE	SUN	SATURN	SQUARE	VENUS
SATURN	CONJUNCT	MARS	SATURN	CONJUNCT	SATURN
URANUS	SQUARE	SUN	URANUS	SEXTILE	VENUS
URANUS	CONJUNCT	URANUS			
NEPTUNE	CONJUNCT	MOON	NEPTUNE	SEXTILE	MERCURY
NEPTUNE	CONJUNCT	NEPTUNE	NEPTUNE	SEXTILE	PLUTO
PLUTO	TRINE	SUN	PLUTO	SEXTILE	MOON
PLUTO	TRINE	MERCURY	PLUTO	SQUARE	VENUS
PLUTO	SEXTILE	NEPTUNE	PLUTO	CONJUNCT	PLUTO

planets, three in Scorpio and one in Pisces. The strong negative preponderance suggests a receptive and intuitive person, perhaps too introverted. The fixed quality, however, provides strength of character and determination. The water element finally lends extra intensity to the emotions. In the table on p. 55, you can see that the fixed quality and the water element are the constituents of the sign of Scorpio. One can tell, therefore, at an early stage, that this chart is strongly coloured by Scorpio, an impression further strengthened by the fact that Pluto, Scorpio's ruler, is in its own sign and also in House VIII, the house traditionally associated with Scorpio.

This is only the first step of the interpretation. Much more information is in store in the listed detailed interpretations in this book. By looking up each entry for the chart you're examining, you'll gather a large number of different character descriptions, most of which will confirm and complement each other.

We shall now return to the sample chart and find some of the different talents, needs and traits indicated by the signs in which the planets appear.

The Sun's place in a birth-chart is the keynote to the person's general character. The other planets strike different chords.

The Sun in Pisces: (p. 129) You live with the guidance of instinct and intuition and occasionally find reality just a little too harsh and prosaic for your taste – unless you've chosen to conform completely with social expectations. You're unselfish by nature and don't mind sacrificing yourself for those worse off. Unfortunately you're very impressionable and tend to run with the hare and hunt with the hounds. Such behaviour is regarded by stronger characters as insincere and deceitful. Under normal circumstances, you're only too ready to yield to more forceful people, suppressing your own impulses, but in a crisis you become unbelievably stubborn and absurdly unreasonable. Most of the time, though, you're affable, easy-going, cheerful and lovable. In love you're romantic, kind, sympathetic and affectionate, but your weak character could lead to promiscuity. Your tendency to escapism could make you addicted to alcohol or drugs.

The Moon in Capricorn (pp. 132–133) is stern, a difficult position which in extreme cases leads to depression, brooding and alcoholism. You are practical and sensible but find it hard to enjoy life. Ambition, hard work and worldly success are your main sources of inner security and often take over the rôle of love: in your eyes, an eminent position compensates for a lot. You are indeed very capable when it comes to administering, organizing and inspiring confidence. Only you know how insecure you really are at heart. Try to show your affection more demonstratively and consider the feelings of others. Did your mother have no time for you as a child?

Mercury in Aquarius (p. 136) is future-orientated and socially aware, fascinated by research and science (in particular social sciences and technology). When it comes to judging other people's character, you're both perceptive and sympathetic, at the same time showing a healthy lack of illusions. You rarely become emotionally involved but are loyal and faithful to both friends and partner. You're most at home in a group of some kind and probably belong to some ideological organization. Controversial discussions stimulate you. Your social conscience is more active that most.

Venus in Aquarius (pp. 139–140) is detached but shows a true humanitarian. In close relationships you insist on retaining your independence. You're not particularly warm or demonstrative, but strange and bizarre love affairs seem inevitable. You either marry young, get divorced and remarry later, or remain single for some time. You're a very good judge of character and extremely tolerant regarding other people's weaknesses. Because of that you have friends in all strata of society. You also have a healthy attitude to money.

Mars in Scorpio (p. 142) is dignified and reserved. You possess an enormous amount of dammed-up energy which screams for an outlet. The channel you usually choose for it is sex: your desires and passions are extremely strong. If sexual conquests are not enough to satisfy you, you may seize upon other means to gain power over others: emotions, cunning, cruelty, violence, aggression, brutality. Once you've set your

97

aim, you will strive towards it, regardless of the expense. In order to avoid destructivity, which in the long run will harm yourself as well as others, you should try to externalize your strong emotional and physical needs and find a spiritual outlet for your sharp, penetrating intellect.

The sign position of the planets shows the different constituents of a personality. The aspects between them, on the other hand, and their activation of different houses, reveal how these manifest themselves.

Of the many aspects given on the data card, we shall examine just a few, such as the Moon's conjunction with Jupiter and Neptune, and also the Sun sextile the Moon. On p. 169 we read that the Sun in soft aspect to the Moon makes a person sincere, loyal, harmonious and responsible. On p. 175 we see that the Moon in soft aspect to Jupiter (the conjunction here is soft) breeds love and harmony, making the person kind, helpful and generous. Add to this the Moon's conjunction to Neptune softened by Jupiter (p. 176), which gives charm, style and good taste, plus a fertile imagination, and we can conclude that the combination of Sun in Pisces, the Sun in soft aspect to the Moon, and the Moon in conjunction with Jupiter and Neptune shows a picture of a warm, kind-hearted person, at times perhaps too soft. Moreover, the Sun forms soft aspects to Jupiter, Neptune and Pluto (pp. 170, 172 and 173).

With this new dimension added to the interpretation, we can return to the sign positions on the previous page. Thanks to the information provided by the aspects, we can now be more selective in assessing what potential characteristics are more or less likely to develop. The characteristics expressed by the aspects prevail over those expressed by the planets, since they reveal how the planets' inherent energies find their best expression in each individual case.

At this stage, any references to the so called node can be ignored. The information has been supplied on the data card for the benefit of those who want to go on to more advanced astrological studies, but it has little relevance to a basic interpretation of the kind we are doing here.

2 Your potential

Before you start the more detailed interpretation of your chart, you can, if you like, use a synthesized method to get an idea of your overriding potential. This method investigates the twelve different astrological principles (the Zodiac signs) with the aim of assessing the frequency of each one in your horoscope. Astrological indications can't be read as facts until they've been repeated and confirmed many times over. When you go on to interpret your chart in detail and find the same potentials repeated yet again, you can start to talk about certainty, because in some cases, as with the aspects, there is no statistical reason why they should be.

Usually a birth-chart shows an emphasis on two, three or perhaps four basic themes, which keep reappearing in different guises. This in itself is remarkable. My own chart, for example, has no fewer than nineteen repetitions of one theme, eighteen of another and ten of a third. The other nine principles appear only once or twice. It is interesting to note, on the other hand, that each theme seems to appear at least once – in other words, all the twelve principles of astrology are present in every chart, although most of them are strictly limited. But each one of us carries the whole of the Zodiac, all the twelve principles, within him or herself. The natal chart and, especially, this investigation illustrate their internal distribution and relationship, pointing out where in the Zodiac our energy is most concentrated and effective.

It's all very simple: go through the following questionnaire, using your data card for reference, and answer all the questions in it. Each 'yes' scores one point, unless otherwise indicated. When you're finished, count the score for each theme. The highest score is your strongest potential. Read the description of the dominating ones on pp. 108–123.

With which planets did you originally feel related? (p. 41) Were they the planets mentioned with the description of your dominant potentials? If not – what could the reason be? I have seen cases where people were extremely attracted to the potentials that were most poorly represented in their charts. All the things lacking in themselves.

From the potential, go on to page 124.

Theme 1

Do you have any of the following in HOUSE I?

Mars?
The Sun?
The Moon?
Ascendant's ruler?
A *strongly* placed planet? (1 point for each)
Two or more planets? (1 point for each)

Do you have any of the following in Aries?

Mars?
The Sun?
The Moon?
The Ascendant?
a *strongly* placed planet? (1 point for each)
Two or more planets? (1 point for each)

Is your Mars in aspect to the Sun or Moon? (1 point for each)
Is your Mars within 10° of the Ascendant or Midheaven?
Do you have a preponderance of fire?
Do you have a preponderance of cardinal signs?
Do you have a preponderance of conjunctions?

Theme 2

Do you have any of the following in HOUSE II?

Venus?
The Sun?
The Moon?
Ascendant's ruler?
A *strongly* placed planet? (1 point for each)
Two or more planets? (1 point for each)

Do you have any of the following in Taurus?

Venus?
The Sun?
The Moon?
The Ascendant?
A *strongly* placed planet? (1 point for each)
Two or more planets? (1 point for each)

Is your Venus in aspect to your Sun or Moon? (1 point for each)
Is your Venus within 10° of the Ascendant or Midheaven?
Do you have a preponderance of earth?
Do you have a preponderance of fixed signs?
Is your score for this theme higher than six? (1 extra point)

Theme 3

Do you have any of the following in HOUSE III?

Mercury?
The Sun?
The Moon?
Ascendant's ruler?
A *strongly* placed planet? (1 point for each)
Two or more planets? (1 point for each)

Do you have any of the following in Gemini?

Mercury?
The Sun?
The Moon?
The Ascendant?
A *strongly* placed planet? (1 point for each)
Two or more planets? (1 point for each)

Is your Mercury in aspect to the Sun or Moon? (1 point for each)
Is your Mercury within 10° of the Ascendant or Midheaven?
Do you have a preponderance of air?
Do you have a preponderance of mutable signs?
Do you have a preponderance of sextiles?

Theme 4

Do you have any of the following in HOUSE IV?

The Moon? (2 points)
The Sun?
Ascendant's ruler?
A *strongly* placed planet (1 point for each)
Two or more planets? (1 point for each)

Do you have any of the following in Cancer?

The Moon? (2 points)
The Sun?
The Ascendant?
A *strongly* placed planet? (1 point for each)
Two or more planets? (1 point for each)

Is your Moon in aspect to your Sun? (2 points)
Is your Moon within 10° of the Ascendant or Midheaven?
Do you have a preponderance of water?
Do you have a preponderance of cardinal signs?
Do you have a preponderance of squares?

Theme 5

Do you have any of the following in HOUSE V?

The Sun? (2 points)
The Moon?
Ascendant's ruler?
A *strongly* placed planet? (1 point for each)
Two or more planets? (1 point for each)

Do you have any of the following in Leo?

The Sun? (2 points)
The Moon?
The Ascendant?
A *strongly* placed planet? (1 point for each)
Two or more planets? (1 point for each)

Is your Sun in aspect to the Moon? (2 points)
Is the Sun within 10° of the Ascendant or Midheaven?
Do you have a preponderance of fire?
Do you have a preponderance of fixed signs?
Do you have a preponderance of trines?

Theme 6

Do you have any of the following in HOUSE VI?

Mercury?
The Sun?
The Moon?
Ascendant's ruler?
A *strongly* placed planet? (1 point for each)
Two or more planets? (1 point for each)

Do you have any of the following in Virgo?

Mercury?
The Sun?
The Moon?
The Ascendant?
A *strongly* placed planet? (1 point for each)
Two or more planets? (1 point for each)

Is your Mercury in aspect to the Sun or Moon? (1 point for each)
Is your Mercury within 10° of the Ascendant or Midheaven?
Do you have a preponderance of earth?
Do you have a preponderance of mutable signs?
Is your score for this theme higher than six? (1 extra point)

Theme 7

Do you have any of the following in HOUSE VII?

Venus?
The Sun?
The Moon?
Ascendant's ruler?

A *strongly* placed planet? (1 point for each)
Two or more planets? (1 point for each)

Do you have any of the following in Libra?

Venus?
The Sun?
The Moon?
The Ascendant?
A *strongly* placed planet? (1 point for each)
Two or more planets? (1 point for each)

Is your Venus in aspect to the Sun or Moon? (1 point for each)
Is your Venus within 10° of the Ascendant or Midheaven?
Do you have a preponderance of air?
Do you have a preponderance of cardinal signs?
Do you have a preponderance of oppositions?

Theme 8

Do you have any of the following in HOUSE VIII?

Mars or Pluto? (½ point for each)
The Sun?
The Moon?
Ascendant's ruler?
A *strongly* placed planet? (1 point for each)
Two or more planets? (1 point for each)

Do you have any of the following in Scorpio?

Mars or Pluto (½ point for each)
The Sun?
The Moon?
The Ascendant?
A *strongly* placed planet? (1 point for each)
Two or more planets? (1 point for each)

Is your Mars or Pluto in aspect to the Sun? (½ point for each)
Is your Mars or Pluto in aspect to the Moon? (½ point for each)

Are your Mars and Pluto in aspect to each other?
Is your Mars or Pluto within 10° of the Ascendant or Midheaven? (½ point for each)
Do you have a preponderance of water?
Do you have a preponderance of fixed signs?
Is your score for this theme higher than six? (1 point extra)

Theme 9

Do you have any of the following in HOUSE IX?

Jupiter?
The Sun?
The Moon?
Ascendant's ruler?
A *strongly* placed planet? (1 point for each)
Two or more planets? (1 point for each)

Do you have any of the following in Sagittarius?

Jupiter?
The Sun?
The Moon?
The Ascendant?
A *strongly* placed planet? (1 point for each)
Two or more planets? (1 point for each)

Is your Jupiter in aspect to the Sun or Moon? (1 point for each)
Is your Jupiter within 10° of the Ascendant or Midheaven?
Do you have a preponderance of fire?
Do you have a preponderance of mutable signs?
Do you have a preponderance of trines?

Theme 10

Do you have any of the following in HOUSE X?

Saturn?
The Sun?
The Moon?

Ascendant's ruler?
A *strongly* placed planet? (1 point for each)
Two or more planets? (1 point for each)

Do you have any of the following in Capricorn?

Saturn?
The Sun?
The Moon?
The Ascendant?
A *strongly* placed planet? (1 point for each)
Two or more planets? (1 point for each)

Is your Saturn in aspect to the Sun or Moon? (1 point for each)
Is your Saturn within 10° of the Ascendant or Midheaven?
Do you have a preponderance of earth?
Do you have a preponderance of cardinal signs?
Do you have a preponderance of squares?

Theme 11

Do you have any of the following in HOUSE XI?

Uranus or Saturn? (½ point for each)
The Sun?
The Moon?
Ascendant's ruler?
A *strongly* placed planet? (1 point for each)
Two or more planets? (1 point for each)

Do you have any of the following in Aquarius?

Uranus or Saturn? (½ point for each)
The Sun?
The Moon?
The Ascendant?
A *strongly* placed planet? (1 point for each)
Two or more planets? (1 point for each)

Is your Uranus or Saturn in aspect to the Sun? (½ point for each)

Is your Uranus or Saturn in aspect to the Moon? (½ point for each)
Are your Uranus and Saturn in aspect to each other?
Is your Uranus or Saturn within 10° of the Ascendant or Midheaven? (½ point for each)
Do you have a preponderance of air?
Do you have a preponderance of fixed signs?
Do you have a preponderance of sextiles?

Theme 12

Do you have any of the following in HOUSE XII?

Neptune or Jupiter? (½ point for each)
The Sun?
The Moon?
Ascendant's ruler?
A *strongly* placed planet? (1 point for each)
Two or more planets? (1 point for each)

Do you have any of the following in Pisces?

Neptune or Jupiter? (2 points for each)
The Sun?
The Moon?
The Ascendant?
A *strongly* placed planet? (1 point for each)
Two or more planets? (1 point for each)

Is your Neptune or Jupiter in aspect to the Sun? (½ point for each)
Is your Neptune or Jupiter in aspect to the Moon? (½ point for each)
Are your Neptune and Jupiter in aspect to each other?
Is your Neptune or Jupiter within 10° of the Ascendant or Midheaven? (½ point for each)
Do you have a preponderance of water?
Do you have a preponderance of mutable signs?
Is your score for this theme higher than six? (1 point extra)

Potential 1

Aries – Mars

" 'Tis better to have fought and lost, than never to have fought at all."

Clough

You are one of the world's pioneers. New ideas are born through you. You're bold and enthusiastic, a good leader and social reformer, always happy to change old conditions and initiate new projects. If you brought your enterprises to a satisfactory conclusion, you would be very useful indeed, but unfortunately this is seldom the case. Besides, you have a destructive side and a certain attraction to violence and aggression. No one would doubt your kinship with Mars, the war god. This also brings other, more appealing traits, such as indomitable courage and invincible faith in your own resources. You belong on a battlefield and could risk your life for fame and glory – as long as you're first in command.

In action, as well as in speech, you attack often and directly. You're impulsive and immediate in your reactions. But your spontaneous, rash response is often ill-considered. You are one of these people who do not look before you leap, and you can be both foolhardy and overdaring. All decisions are made on the spur of the moment, and it would never occur to you to seek advice first. On the other hand, you often know better than many others, and you're often ahead of time.

In most things you go to extremes. Others may get the impression that you're untruthful, because you love to improve on a story and exaggerate – especially to glorify your own person. But one couldn't accuse you of being a liar. And when you bully others, it's not with the object of putting them down – just of asserting yourself.

You're more quarrelsome and irritable than most and frequently blow your top, even if your bad temper doesn't last long. Endurance and patience are not among your main assets, and you could be very restless. With your fiery nature you are sexy and passionate, but you seem to enjoy the chase more than the conquest – a principle which could, incidentally, be applied to most of your enterprises. Several marriages are likely – as usual you're too rash when it comes to making important decisions, and you allow yourself to be carried away by desire.

Headaches and fever may be a problem. And your reckless nature make you accident-prone. Your general welfare is constantly on the way up or down. But don't complain: permanent success would soon bore you stiff – what you want is action. If the variation and excitement don't arrive by themselves, you soon think of some way of bringing them about.

With your great originating powers, it's a pity that so much of your plentiful energy is wasted in the pursuit of personal gratification. You have so much to offer other people, once you stop thinking only of yourself.

Potential 2

Taurus – Venus

'Where your treasure is, there will your heart be also.'
Matthew 6:21

You are a pillar of society. With every breath you draw, you lay your foundation for the future, with a carefully considered plan in mind. Your economy is as stable as you are yourself. You're reliable and trustworthy and follow, on the whole, convention. You realize the value of accepted standards and are happy as long as there are rules you can abide by and authorities to obey. Without them you'd feel very insecure. But take care not to become dogmatic.

Your practical, earthbound nature does not like change and adventure – everyday routine is fine for you, and you aim towards a regular, methodical life. Few people have your industry, perseverance and determination.

Material things, or possessions as such, could play a symbolic role in your life for all the things you appreciate, security in particular. All beautiful things appeal to you – including scenery, music and art. You may be a collector or have an artistic talent of your own, in which case you're most likely to sing or paint. Your sense of form is acute.

If you're an artist – indeed, whatever vocation you choose – you'll be very productive as long as you're motivated. You possess great resources of hidden strength. Unfortunately, your energy often remains dormant, due to a tendency to indolence and inertia. Don't let yourself be inhibited by your own body and your obsession with well-being. Where health is concerned, your throat is most at risk.

You are likely to marry young after a period of intense, purposeful courtship. Marriage satisfies your need for a settled life, which in your terms means a comfortable, beautiful home, good food on the table, sexual security and the affection and devotion of a family. You are kind, sensitive and sensual with a highly developed sense of touch. You need to be physically close to those you love and like to touch other people when you talk to them – even when you stop a stranger in the street to ask for directions.

Your sense of humour is earthy and hearty, not to say raucous. It flourishes under extra stimulation. If you can manage to raise your material need for beauty from a consuming to a creative level, you will find that it serves you rather than limits you. Don't let your acquisitive streak make you mean.

Potential 3

Gemini – Mercury

'Absence of occupation is not rest; a mind quite vacant is a mind distressed.'

Cowper

You are a catalyst – the connecting link between people and ideas. With your propensity for indentification and classi-fication, you're very well suited for passing on information. Words are your medium – they bring order to the chaos in your brain: its throng of thoughts, ideas, impulses and impressions.

You like to fill your life with interesting new experiences; your curiosity and your craving for change and stimulation are insatiable. Consequently, you often suffer from frustration and discontent. It may not have occurred to you that a shortcut to greater satisfaction would be to delve into just one subject more deeply, to enjoy it more.

You learn easily and probably did well at school – at least to begin with. In the later stages of education, your lack of application and concentration may have been a handicap. You have a good ear for languages and good business acumen.

People like you seldom devote themselves to anything in life. Imitating comes to you more easily than originating, even in the literal sense of the word: you could be a splendid mimic. When you're not having 'fun' – that is, when you, like the rest of us, have to subject yourself to a certain routine and discipline – you become depressed. You have a surplus of nervous energy, which you dissipate with unnecessary gestures and movements. You may find it particularly difficult to keep hands and feet still.

Just as you rarely stick to one project at a time, your circle of friends includes a multitude of different people. In love you change partners quite often. If someone tries to tie you down, you become restless and evasive. Independence and experience mean more to you than love and affection. You can be both hard and selfish in emotional relations.

Your quick wit and repartee make you amusing and stimulating to have around. But your great talent for verbal expression is a constant temptation to abuse. You know that you can easily persuade others, and you're not usually bothered by scruples. Another fault of yours is a tendency to lying and gossiping, to talking yourself out of difficult situations, with scant regard for the truth of the matter. You may also try to impress others with empty boasting or promises. Or are you one of those who talk just for the sake of it, who always keep chattering about nothing, as if silence was something to be abhorred?

There is no excuse for your weaknesses – they can so easily be avoided. All you have to do is take an interest in other people and their feelings and learn to listen as well as you talk.

Potential 3

Cancer – Moon

'All of man's misfortunes are due to the fact that he doesn't practise the art of remaining in his room.'

Pascal

You are like a mirror constantly reflecting your surroundings: your great sensitivity magnifies what appears around you, giving it unforeseen dimensions. As long as the true proportions are not distorted, this ability of yours can have a profoundly beneficial effect on the world in which you live.

You're a receptive person with a strong intuition and a fertile imagination. Your environment has a profound effect on you – one could even say that it provides your identity. No wonder your surroundings are of such paramount importance to you. You spend – or would like to spend – a great deal of your life within your own four walls, where you make a great effort to create comfort and ease. Your home provides you with the security you can't do without; once you step outside, you become defensive and reserved. Although nothing frightens you more than the prospect of rejection, ridicule or hurt feelings (you're certainly quick to take offence!), you yourself can be very intolerant and disapproving to people outside your immediate circle.

You like to be a focal figure in your family. Within the safe framework of the home you can also give free rein to your intense, highly strung emotions. You compensate for your own feelings of insecurity and timidity by dominating other members of your family. You confirm your hold over them by regular emotional confrontations. If they oppose you in this, your reaction is that of a martyr given to self-pity.

In official situations, on the other hand, you're diplomatic, sensible, responsible and patriotic. You're loyal to authority, because you see the established society (or state, or monarchy) as a provider of security. Your memory for historical events is remarkable. As a teacher you have an opportunity to let your best sides flourish in the service of society. You tend to grow with the demands that are made upon you, and may thus surprise both yourself and others.

112

In love, you're romantic and devoted but shy and passive. Your feelings are warm and active and you're not afraid of commitment. If it turns out that your partner does not return your love, or if he/she disappoints you, your love will change into a strongly protective, possibly indulgent, form of tenderness, which craves no tribute. Perhaps it's as a parent that you have most to offer – as long as you don't use the parental rôle to assert your own identity, regardless of the child's special needs.

Your weakest point is your temperament – you can be moody, capricious, childish, petty and unreasonable, whenever you feel like it. Those closest to you are usually the target of your bad temper. If you use your sensitivity to inspire others rather than indulge in exaggerated emotions, both you and your loved ones will fare better.

Potential 5

Leo – Sun

(The vixen taunted the lioness for having had only one cub, when she herself had had five.) The lioness replied: 'One – but a lion.'

Aesop

You need to have a constant outlet for your force and vitality. Without ample opportunity to project yourself onto your environment, you perish. The risk of this happening is, by all means, rarely impending, because your undoubted authority and flair for organization usually lead to great achievements. You're able to influence both public opinion and people in power, and it would be surprising if you were not successful in life. Your close relations the Sun and Leo (the sign of kings) give you a generous measure of enthusiasm and magnanimity. You enjoy pomp and splendour and all kinds of drama – especially when the leading rôle is reserved for yourself.

You're likely to have a strong build and a deep, resounding voice. Your energy level is high and you radiate warmth – even your body temperature is often above normal. You're good-hearted, generous, lofty, loyal and affectionate. You love the world as much as you love yourself, and assume optimistically that all other people share your high ethical ideals. You need no reminder that your principle of trusting everyone leads to regular disappointments. You seem to be the worst judge of character in the world. Or is it only a stubborn refusal to accept any lack of integrity in man?

In a direct conflict with another person, you can be very persistent and obdurate, as long as you're convinced you're in the right. However, faced with facts, you will graciously bow – on one condition: that your dignity is left intact. You never give up your prestige without a fight. But provided your opponent knows how to handle you, you're an easy person to come to terms with. Still, your first responsibility is always to yourself, and as long as you're doing what you consider to be correct, you're not worried by opposition from the rest of the world.

The thing you should watch out for is a tendency to self-glorification and conceit. Try to check any smugness, arrogance and condescension in your relations with others. Don't bask in flattery but take it for what it's worth. And remember that the humble will inherit the earth.

Potential 6

Virgo – Mercury

'Do your duty, and leave the rest to the gods.'

Corneille

Without you, the world would be in chaos. All its wretched untidy, disorganized people would be lost without your assistance, without your sense of order and regularity, without your solutions to irksome problems. You're a born strategist, excellent at handling other people's affairs, personally or professionally, asked or unasked. Sometimes you indulge in pure manipulation, but even then your intentions are above reproach.

You're quite happy to supply your services from a background position, and you're an ideal ministering spirit: discreet, loyal, dutiful, faithful and reliable. You don't mind working hard or for long hours. In your opinion, if a thing is worth doing, it's worth doing properly. With each detail scrupulously attended to. The results you achieve are naturally good, within the limits of your ability. If you could refrain from analysing, criticizing and pulling them to pieces, you might even enjoy them a little.

Your vocation is important to you and always involves service to others. The medical profession would suit you very well. Have you ever contemplated being a doctor or nurse? For a sick person nothing could be more comfortable and reassuring than the touch of your capable, careful, considerate and conscientious hands. Your nearest and dearest also have good reason to appreciate your talent at looking after other people – but unfortunately, they often make the mistake of taking it for granted.

It's a pity that your own personal life so often becomes a mess. The standards you apply to yourself are so high that they threaten to stifle you. If you can't do a thing with one hundred per cent perfection, you prefer not to do it at all. That way you miss many opportunities, and your life becomes sadly limited. As a consequence you may develop a mean, frustrated, destructive and overly critical attitude towards other people, whose apparent success and freedom you envy. Your bad moods will then become your own worst enemy.

Make a conscious effort to think positively and to exploit your best potential. Apart from the approval you deserve and receive from society, you have been well endowed by life: you're clever, with highly developed and exact powers of expression, and a nice, dry sense of humour. When you relax, you develop a very special charm. Your manners are impeccable and your emotions well mastered. You're likely to have fine features and always dress well. Isn't that enough to develop and enjoy?

Potential 7

Libra – Venus

'No one exists alone.'

Auden

Your rôle in life is that of a mediator. You weigh, balance and judge different aspects of ideas and situations, especially those involving human relations. Your sense of justice is always alert. At the same time you find decision-making difficult, because you're able to see all sides of an issue.

Your diplomatic disposition is an asset in negotiation and speculation and often gives you the upper hand. Your business sense is highly developed. But you prefer to act with a partner, if possible with the support of as many people as possible. Conflicting opinions confuse you.

Because your fellow-man is so important to you, you do your best to get on well with everyone. You are usually quite popular – indeed, you have public appeal and could become a favourite with the masses. On a more personal level, you're very pleasant to have around – you're sensitive to other people's feelings and opinions, cheerful and easy-going, humane and humanistic, witty and helpful. But you do expect the same kind of assistance when you need it – money, for one thing, is freely lent and borrowed. You are both generous and extravagant.

In daily life you may be slightly impatient and untidy, too eager to conclude things properly. You love art and beauty, and you're probably artistic and beautiful yourself. Elegance, style and good taste are your faithful companions.

One thing that disturbs you more than anything else is discord and angry confrontations. To preserve the peace you may sometimes be too keen to forgive and forget. You may even prefer insincerity and hypocrisy to unpleasantness and disharmony. If someone makes you really angry, you say nothing. Another reason why you often shut your eyes instead of clearing the air is your inability to function alone. A close partnership is as vital to you as the air you breathe. If you should suddenly find yourself without a close relationship with another person, that equilibrium you always strive for abandons you completely. Your whole being is shattered inside out and you're likely to do something desperate. But don't panic! You were made for relating to others, your balance will soon be restored, it will come from within, it's part of yourself. Very soon, a new involvement will replace the one you lose.

You're a devoted lover, and although you can't help being aware of the attraction of other beautiful creatures, you would be foolish to risk a precious ongoing relationship by infidelity. Keep this in mind and don't give your weakness a chance! You yourself can be jealous – even without reason! You certainly don't like the idea of losing the one you love.

If you manage to satisfy your craving for beauty and pleasure on an artistic level, you'll reduce the risk of decadence.

Potential 8

Scorpio – Mars and Pluto

'Great ruins make way for greater glories.'

Seneca

Provided you can find a social or creative outlet for your tremendous inner strength, you have great resources to influence or transform the world. The decision how you should best serve society is up to yourself and your conscience. There is always a temptation to abuse power like yours.

To safeguard your own sense of security, you like to have control of both people and situations. You're purposeful and determined and hold on to the course you've set for yourself, undaunted by warnings or obstacles. But it's essential that this iron will of yours finds a positive outlet, because your compelling nature could become dangerous and destructive if directed inwards towards yourself or to some other person. Woe betide whoever opposes you. You can be cruel and brutal, revengeful and unscrupulous.

You're often only vaguely aware of the strong power you possess – and it frightens you more than any external threat ever could. Much too often you protect yourself against it by

117

denying it and repressing feelings and impulses. But that is not a solution. Your strength is there because the world needs it – and properly used, it could never hurt either you or anyone else.

You have intense likes and dislikes and certainly make your mark on your environment. In the home you could be a tyrant. You attract the opposite sex and are yourself strongly attracted by it. Promiscuity is one possible way of coping with surplus energy, but you'll find that this does little to fulfil your strong emotional needs. Your powerful sex drive is an expression of a deep yearning to merge with another person, body and soul. It's a pity that you often use it as a tool to gain control over your partner. This will never satisfy you, and it only serves to repel the other person. To find peace, you must go beyond desire and discover love.

Your best sides flourish when you apply yourself to improving existing social conditions. You like to investigate things beneath the surface; with your great powers of perception, you read signs other people don't even notice. Thus you have a lot of secret information available to you, and could make a successful sleuth – or criminal. You choose. Danger doesn't put you off.

Your sharp wit and shrewd sarcastic comments, usually dead on target, are as amusing as they are cruel, depending on the victim. This is another instance where your astute mind would be more honourably applied to social reformation rather than to attacking weak, defenceless creatures.

Potential 9

Sagittarius – Jupiter

'By improving yourself, you improve the world. Any argument against it is an excuse.'

AH

You carry the banner of faith – if nothing else, in the form of a positive outlook on life. This serves as a good example for your more pessimistic fellow-men – especially since you seem to do quite well for yourself. This may surprise others more than you. You happily assume that help will turn up just at the moment when it's needed – and that's exactly what happens in your case.

This conviction that everything will turn out for the best is in fact a sign of religiosity or at least philosophy. You may choose a different term for it, but the basis is the same. It also shows in your judgement, which is sound and profound, and you become wiser as you get older, more so than other people. Professional counselling would suit you. In some instances you're almost prophetic.

For most of the time, you're involved in one project or other, aiming at self-improvement of some kind. You have an insatiable appetite for new experiences and fresh knowledge. You enjoy life and you're adventurous, impulsive and youthful throughout life. Outdoor life appeals to you, you're athletic and like to take an active part in sports, often equestrian sports, because you love animals. But don't be reckless: even your luck has its bounds, and there is a risk of accidents. You also devote yourself to calmer pursuits, possibly at the expense of the others: you have many humanistic and academic interests – literature in particular.

There is a tendency to dissipate energy – you like to shoot off arrows in all directions, not even bothering to check where the target is, or if it exists. You're magnanimous, benevolent and good-natured. Sometimes, to your amazement, you may be accused of insincerity. That's when people who lack your naturally jovial disposition attach too much significance to your exuberance and then feel that you fail to live up to your promises. You are equally astonished when people are hurt by your straightforward remarks. No one could bear less malice than you.

Still, it takes a lot to make you really unpleasant. That only happens when your liberty and independence are at stake, for without them you know you'd perish. In spite of this, it confuses you when your relationships and marriages fail, and you could become very cynical and bitter. But someone like you, who regards home life and marriage as a starting-point rather than a purpose in life, can't expect to have your cake and eat it. You're passionate and ardent enough – but at heart you're the eternal bachelor or bachelor girl.

Potential 10

Capricorn – Saturn

'Let us then be up and doing, with a heart for any fate; Still achieving, still pursuing, learn to labour and to wait.'

Longfellow

You like to further your worldly aims and give them concrete, practical application. In doing so, you exert a stabilizing influence on the world. You're diligent and industrious and prefer having each thing in its proper place.

Parental and, later in life, social approval is essential to you, and you provide the security you need by your own achievements. Personal ambition is an integrated part of your nature, and you had better choose fields of activity where this is regarded as an asset. Team work is not for you – you would never even think of interfering in other people's affairs, and certainly wouldn't tolerate any meddling in your own. Besides, you're a loner at heart, and your timid, reserved character would find it hard to assert itself in a group situation. But in a responsible position you will soon be respected and admired for your ability, which conceals any tendencies to snobbery or social climbing.

You flourish in an authoritative job where you can devote yourself to administration and organization. You're very good at solving problems, particularly mathematical ones. You have the memory of an elephant and a good head for figures.

With your thrifty, economical disposition, it's inevitable that you gradually accumulate wealth. The type of safe and sound investment that appeals to you most is property, primarily your own home. You happily provide any financial and material assets your family may need, but in return you demand respect and loyalty from them.

You're a serious person and should try to be less severe, restrained, melancholy and depressive. Your deep thoughts are often reflected by deep-set eyes and a sombre look. On the surface, on the other hand, you can be amusing and easy-going. Many people are surprised by your unexpected caprices.

You're quite conventional in love and marriage, which you regard as a necessary social institution. You're loyal and faithful but not particularly warm or affectionate to your spouse, who may find you overly possessive.

As a parent you could be very strict. Your own parents probably expected a lot from you. You've never been young at heart, but remember it's never too late!

Potential 11

Aquarius – Uranus and Saturn

'The truth shall make you free.'

John 8:32

You believe in humanitarian ideals and do your best to co-ordinate the rest of mankind. Without you and your brethren, membership in ideological organizations would be down significantly. The modern social sciences with the focus on man – psychology, sociology, anthropology – are your domain. You're not only a good teacher of these subjects but also an excellent therapist, with a soothing effect on troubled minds. You look to other people for experience, rather than to books and situations, convinced that everyone has something of value to teach. Your great tolerance, broad mind and lack of prejudice help you see other human beings exactly as they are, with all their faults and shortcomings. Being a sincere researcher, you're only looking for one thing: the truth.

Your thought patterns are clear, concise and systematic. This is perhaps the reason why more confused creatures can't understand you. Nothing could make you more frustrated. Another explanation is that your unconventional, independent outlook on life is simply beyond some people's comprehension. All things are relative, but those who call you eccentric, rebellious or anarchistic may not be all that far out.

Your free, unfettered mind is ideal for scientific purposes. You're clever at inventing and renewing, especially in the field of electronics and other advanced technology. If you have artistic leanings, you are sure to be a modernist. Your ability to gather many people under one flag also makes you an excellent leader of large organizations, preferably of a humanitarian kind.

You're seldom found alone – you work best in a team. As a friend you're loyal and faithful, open and honest – until someone makes demands of even greater openness. Then you'll clam up like a shell. You won't let anyone interfere with your mental processes!

Although you are basically impersonal, cool and detached, you can be very attractive. You may use your power of attraction in a rather unscrupulous manner. As far as your own feelings go, your sense of moderation is an efficient antidote to rapture; unfortunately that means you miss out on some of life's most beautiful moments. Let's hope you come to terms with this – before they have all passed!

Potential 12

Pisces – Neptune and Jupiter

'Do good by stealth, and blush to find it fame.'

Pope

You are a great philanthropist, without a trace of self-interest. Your sympathy, compassion and mercy are almost self-effacing. Without hesitation, you turn the other cheek when smitten. But how can a kind, trusting, impressionable person like you survive in a hard world? Doesn't it eat you alive?

Certain things come to your assistance: to begin with, your instinct, receptivity and sensitivity to other people's feelings, which take you further than ever logic or senses ever would. There is also your deep love of mankind, which gives you the strength to work indefatigably under difficult conditions, as long as you know that it's for the benefit of someone else. But then there are problems: your will is weak, and you're unpractical, changeable, indecisive and easily led astray. Your dreamy, unworldly outlook may strengthen your spirit, but it's not much use when it comes to sheer survival. On the contrary – your yearning for peace and fulfilment could induce you to reject reality, possibly with the help of alcohol or drugs. If you're lucky, you have an artistic streak; that should be cultivated to attain spiritual satisfaction through your own creative achievements.

You have many advantages over other people, though you may not think so yourself. For one thing, you adjust easily. In artistic work, your inspiration is almost visionary. And your great talent for empathy makes you not only a sympathetic listener but also a skilful mimic and a good actor. However, your weak ego may tempt you to abuse these qualities and instead be insincere, hypocritical, untruthful and perfidious. Don't let external influences confuse you and don't let yourself down in order to please others! Try to be as sincere intellectually as you are emotionally.

You cry easily, even – or especially – on other people's behalf. You may be carried away by pity and become maudlin and sentimental. In love you're romantic and dedicated, unable to see any faults in your partner. You could also be promiscuous, because you're extremely weak where love is concerned. Still, given the choice, you prefer to love spiritually as well as erotically, and you protect your feelings from any crudeness or vulgarity.

If you really want to go through life without sacrificing any of your integrity, you must learn to assert yourself more genuinely. The best way to do that is by a humanitarian contribution of some kind. There is certainly a demand for you in this world, which has so much suffering and so many people who, unlike you, remain indifferent to the plight of their fellow-human beings.

3 Interpreting the planets

Having established your potential, you now know what sort of traits the more detailed interpretation of your chart ought to confirm. First of all, make a general examination of your chart. Assess the distribution of positive and negative planets, as well as the frequency of each quality and element. Go back to the sign division (pp. 46–56) if you have forgotten the implications of this. This information is a good introduction to the interpretation of your chart. Does it tie in with the potential you have just uncovered?

Now you can go on to the interpretation of your Sunsign (pp. 125–129). Then read the Sunsign interpretation for the sign on your Ascendant (the significance of the Ascendant is explained on p. 58). After that, read the sign interpretation for the Moon and the planets in turn (pp. 130–152). Then go on to the interpretation of the house position of each body (pp. 153–166), as you see it on your data card. (If you have forgotten the significance of planets and houses, these are described on pp. 37–41 and pp. 64–65 respectively.)

Also bear in mind the *placing* of each planet (p. 73) when you read the interpretation. If a planet is very *softly* placed, i.e. forming several *soft* aspects, its full potential may still be dormant – but if you're lucky, it's already flourishing. If a planet is very *hard* placed, there is a risk that its destructive tendencies might dominate, unless you've already learnt to control that difficult side of your character.

From the planets, go on to page 167.

Planets in different signs: *The Sun*

The Sun in Aries: You are not troubled by inhibition – you rush in, bold and hopeful, always delighted to find a new channel for your boundless energy. The worst thing that could happen to you would be not to have any new projects to attack. If you were equally zealous when it came to completing things, you would go far – but results don't really count for you. Your keen, aggressive, competitive mind flourishes when challenged – professionally, intellectually or – indeed – emotionally. You are ardent and passionate. In most situations, your attitude is one of 'me first', but your enthusiasm is contagious, and you will inspire others to follow you. Therefore the term of leader is more fair than that of egotist – as long as your initiative does not deteriorate into ruthless self-assertion at the expense of others. You can be very thoughtless, even cruel.

The Sun in Taurus: You are a peaceful nature – until the limit of your great patience has been reached. The soft surface hides an iron will, or the opposite: a rough surface hides a heart of gold. You're not very receptive and find it difficult to accept opinions differing from your own. With perseverance and endurance you apply yourself to the tasks given to you. You're practical and productive but tend to be slow and phlegmatic. You like to own all things beautiful and all the people you love. Your vast need of security could be fulfilled on a material level. You're devoted to your home (including good food) and your marriage. You're sensuous, loving and affectionate. Your sense of beauty could well be developed artistically. Your throat is somehow in focus – either troubling you with tonsillitis or pleasing others with a beautiful voice.

The Sun in Gemini: You are ruled by your brains – you're intelligent, logical and rational and talk well and profusely. Your active mind constantly moves from one subject to another, and you're always involved in many different interests and activities simultaneously. Don't let yourself be limited by this versatility – try concentrating rather than dissipating your energy. You could be a Jack-of-all-trades who does nothing very well. Another inhibiting factor is your restless and changeable nature. Your curiosity and your craving for new, stimulating experiences keep you youthful and active throughout your life. You assert yourself well in discussions and have a good business sense. On the other hand, your need for constant variation makes you less loyal to friends and lovers. You don't always consider other people's feelings, because your own are rarely profound.

The Sun in Cancer: Your home is your castle. You prefer to play a key rôle in a limited environment which guarantees the protection and comfort you can't do without. You have a tendency to cling to that which provides security: the past, possessions, your home, marriage and family. With your nearest and dearest you flourish – you give them your love freely, without expecting anything in return. Your strongest identity comes to you as a parent. Generally, you're nicer with those who are weak and helpless and don't question your supremacy or your decisions. Cut off from your safe background you feel exposed and vulnerable and keep other people at bay. You're very sensitive and easily hurt, and this can lead to violent emotional scenes, pettiness and un-reasonable behaviour. Most of the time you let your emotions rule, and you can be a slave to your own moods.

The Sun in Leo: You are good-hearted and immensely generous – you give freely of yourself, convinced that this marvellous gift will be appreciated by everyone. Then you're deeply hurt by the receiver's ingratitude, meanness and criticism – reactions which are completely alien to you. But you have a tendency to use other people to show off your own glory – and if this occasionally backfires, you have, in effect, asked for it. Still, your intentions are always good – and you're honest, sincere and genuinely kind. You're a master at delegating disagreeable duties in order to concentrate on the more important, creative (read more amusing) tasks – but then, you probably do them better than anyone else. As long as your self-projection doesn't take over completely, you have a lot to offer the world. Just remember that even the humble are worth listening to – and that receiving is a nobler art that giving.

The Sun in Virgo: You like to take care of others – personally or professionally – yours is the sign of service. Your vocation is important to you and you work conscientiously, method-ically and thoroughly. But don't let your dedicated appli-cation to detail cloud more important issues. You're clever and a quick learner, intellectual and practical, tidy and analytical. Where your private life is concerned, you're hesitant and vacillating, whereas you often help others with good advice and faithful, loyal support. You can give in to self-denial, which comes naturally to you, but if this happens, you develop into a frustrated, over-critical, querulous person, envying others their chances of self-realization. Your love affairs are few and you accept celibacy, but once committed, your feelings are deep and enduring.

The Sun in Libra: Your fellow-men are very important to you – one nice quality is your readiness to share other people's conditions. On the other hand, you could do with a little more independence. You're a very sociable nature, and your worship of all the good things in life includes a considerable portion of good food and drink. Not only that – witty conversation, cultural pursuits and all things beautiful are also part of the necessities, not to mention love. To you, love is indeed the salt of the earth. You need a permanent com-panion, but you don't mind changing partners now and then and could be fairly flirtatious and easy-going. Still, whatever you do is done in style. You're surrounded by an aura of elegance and refinement and hate anything sordid or vulgar. You're charming and popular and co-operative, sometimes to the extent of compromising yourself to avoid a conflict.

The Sun in Scorpio: You are a very determined, strong-willed person who prefers dominating others, in a more or less subtle manner. If you don't succeed in winning them over with your powerful magnetic attraction, which *is* quite hard to resist, you may reach for stronger weapons, such as your astute mind, remarkable perception and sharp tongue, which often indulges in delivering accurate sarcastic remarks. With your innate suspicion, you lead your life as others play poker, and few people can guess what really goes on inside you. You have a forceful, emotionally charged sex drive which increases your hold on your partner. But beware of being too jealous and possessive. You have an inner strength which could lead to grand achievements – provided you direct it out, from yourself! Your admirable powers of self-control can easily turn into unhealthy self-repression.

The Sun in Sagittarius: You take life rather as you find it. With high spirits and unflinching optimism you indulge in a number of different pursuits: interests, hobbies and projects. You're benevolent, good-natured and humorous and will always remain youthful, both physically and mentally. You love adventure, long journeys and new, exciting experiences. Your straightforward manner can occasionally land you in trouble – you could unintentionally be blunt and tactless. In spite of your athletic physique, you're clumsy with material things – perhaps because they're not all that important to you. Your convivial surface goes with a philosophical outlook on life. Your integrity is usually above reproach. All humanistic subjects appeal to you, and you could well have an academic profession. You are wise and give good advice. Your home, family and marriage are of secondary interest.

The Sun in Capricorn: Your ambition is indefatigable. Early in life you decide upon a course and then hold on to it throughout life, working methodically and conscientiously. You're dutiful and tenacious and it's not surprising that, sooner or later, you achieve exactly what you had in mind: usually a responsible, well-paid position in a government department or a large enterprise. You take yourself seriously, but that side of your character may be concealed under a delightful, modest, charming façade, which on suitable occasions develops into pure frivolity. You're given to eager discussion – about anything, as long as it doesn't touch upon your private life. That is something you rather keep to yourself. In love, you're not exactly warm or demonstrative.

Your marriage partner is probably socially suitable and sharing your interest in worldly success.

The Sun in Aquarius: You are what we call a modern person – unconventional and socially aware, progressive and unprejudiced, often actively involved in politics. Traditions and authority mean less to you than liberty, equality, democracy and similar humanitarian ideals. Ideological movements exert the strongest attraction – first and foremost, you're a theorist. Science is another area where you would stand out with your free, inventive mind. But you rarely change your opinions and, in spite of being broad-minded and tolerant, you must watch out for being limited by your own ideals and dogmas. Your attitude to other people is sympathetic but at the same time cool, detached and free from all illusions. This makes you an excellent judge of character. You prefer to merge with a group and do not function well on your own. With friends and marriage partner you're loyal and faithful. You adore wild scenery.

The Sun in Pisces: You live with the guidance of instinct and intuition and occasionally find reality just a little too harsh and prosaic for your taste – unless you've chosen to conform completely with social expectations. You're unselfish by nature and don't mind sacrificing yourself for those worse off. Unfortunately you're very impressionable and tend to run with the hare and hunt with the hounds. Such behaviour is regarded by stronger characters as insincere and deceitful. Under normal circumstances, you're only too ready to yield to more forceful people, suppressing your own impulses, but in a crisis you become unbelievably stubborn and absurdly unreasonable. Most of the time, though, you're affable, easygoing, cheerful and lovable. In love you're romantic, kind, sympathetic and affectionate, but your weak character could lead to promiscuity. Your tendency to escapism could make you addicted to alcohol and drugs.

Planets in different signs: *The Moon*

The Moon in Aries is fiery and alert. You act on instinct, following the call of your senses. Decisions are made on the spur of the moment; your reactions are immediate and astute. Once you stop, you lose your train of thought and concentration – without constant activity you become restless. You have a hot temper and say and do a lot in anger, which you have cause to regret later on. You're independent, headstrong and self-assured and won't take advice from anyone. Your mother was probably a strong character. You're not the faithful type and your marriage is bound to be stormy.

The Moon in Taurus is serene and balanced – a good position. You're reliable, with good powers of concentration. Rash decisions are not for you – you take your time and consider everything carefully before you act, but then it's usually with good results. Try not to be overly stubborn and rigid. You love your family and probably had a happy childhood with an affectionate mother. The prospects for marriage are good – but you should avoid regarding your partner as a possession. You enjoy all the good things in life and attract comfort and wealth. Good food and drink play an important rôle in your life – this could eventually become a problem.

The Moon in Gemini is nervous, restless and changeable. You are intelligent and active in many areas; you read, study and talk intensely but have a tendency to skim the surface of life. Abstract ideas and experiences are easily expressed in words. You don't attach any great importance to emotions – neither your own or those of others, although you enjoy talking about them. You convey impressions well but crave constant intellectual stimulation and variation. Professionally you could be a jack-of-all-trades. You may use your verbal talents to talk yourself out of difficult situations and tell lies without scruples. Your mother was probably intellectually inclined.

The Moon in Cancer is warm and protective, a strong position, which can, however, make you spoilt and idle and inspire the misconception that the world owes you a living.

Your mother is an important figure in your life – have you cut the umbilicial cord yet? You're sensitive and receptive to your environment – you prefer staying in your own home, enjoying the comfort and security it offers. You make a good parent and like to look after those you love, but your passive attitude makes you overly dependent, and you tend to evade responsibility. You have an excellent retentive memory. Try not to give in to your moods!

The Moon in Leo is happy and positive – but dependent on love and approval. You're lucky in that you usually have your way, and people in authority generally support you. The arts or literature could well be your field. Your sense of honour is strong – you tend to keep your promises. Because you're so reliable, you often end up in a responsible position. When it comes to love, you're extremely healthy. You give everything to the one you love – but don't be indiscreet and take good care of your reputation. Make sure you're not inadvertently smug and condescending – that will soon take away the popularity you can't live without. Your mother was probably autocratic.

The Moon in Virgo is practical and economical. You're too much of a worrier and could have nervous stomach trouble. Work means a lot to you – you're analytically inclined, with an excellent memory, and you work diligently and meticulously, seldom complaining. You're modest and unpretentious. Your mother was of the sensible kind. As a child, you were loved only on certain conditions and so you developed into a reserved, disciplined, insecure adult, who never gives free reins to his emotions. Criticism and coldness can repel your partner. The one thing that could give you happiness would be a deep and sincere relationship with another person.

The Moon in Libra is graceful and charming, harmonious and popular. It's a suitable position for diplomats and all professions based on human relations. Your mother was probable well balanced – you generate emotional equilibrium yourself and excel at pouring oil on troubled waters. If a conflict is inevitable, you'll do anything to avoid a direct confrontation, even at the expense of honesty and self-respect. You need beautiful, harmonious surroundings and could be pleasure-seeking. Without a partner taking his (and preferably also your) share of responsibility and decisions, you're hesitant and confused. You have good taste and hate vulgarity.

The Moon in Scorpio is intense. Not the best place for the Moon, which easily becomes angry and resentful here. But you can be as creative as you are destructive: you're perceptive and sure of aim, with fantastic powers of observation and a very special kind of intelligence. Your will is overpowering and you make your mark on others. Where your emotions are concerned, however, you run the risk of drowning in your own desires and developing into a ruthless hedonist using others for sensual gratification. Try to fight your tendency to promiscuity, perversion and dissipation. At the same time, find a constructive outlet for energy and impulses – don't suppress them. Your mother was probably jealous and domineering.

The Moon in Sagittarius is fickle and careless, as well as optimistic and happy-go-lucky. You frequently change your residence and feel restless if you spend too much time in one place. You have a vaguely idealistic streak and a sound judgement. Your mother was probably philosophically inclined but not warm or demonstrative. You are a stimulating and heart-warming companion but not easy to live with, because you accept no limitation of your personal freedom and rarely concentrate on financial or domestic issues. Your easy-going attitude to money makes you constantly indebted.

The Moon in Capricorn is stern, a difficult position which in extreme cases leads to depression, brooding and alcoholism. You are practical and sensible but find it hard to enjoy life. Ambition, hard work and worldly success are your main sources of inner security and often take over the rôle of love: in your eyes, an eminent position compensates for a lot. You are indeed very capable when it comes to administering, organizing and inspiring confidence. Only you know how insecure you really are at heart. Try to show your affection more demonstratively and consider the feelings of others. Did your mother have no time for you as a child?

The Moon in Aquarius is moderate and rational, helpful and humanitarian, but sometimes overly detached and impersonal. You can be quite inventive, but don't go so far that you become eccentric. You have most to offer in a group situation – close relationships give you a feeling of suffocation and you evade individual responsibility. As a friend you're loyal and faithful and you value friendship very highly, but you seem to attract friends who are not much use to you: they may be unreliable, anti-social, eccentric or Bohemian and can cause you great problems. Your best potential is in electronics, scientific research and social sciences.

The Moon in Pisces is vacillating and indecisive. You swing from one emotional extreme to another: from, on the one hand, self-pity and maudlin dependence on your partner to, on the other, warm generosity and self-sacrifice. You're incredibly romantic and completely unrealistic. Anyone could influence you – you keep changing your mind and will go back on your word rather than risk losing popularity. There are probably people in your immediate vicinity who have discovered this and take advantage of it. To escape reality you may go to excess with sex, alcohol and drugs. Your mother probably made great sacrifices for you.

Planets in different signs: *Mercury*

Mercury in Aries is astute and quick at repartee. But your sharp wit often turns into quarrelling and sarcasm which hurt more than you appreciate. You have high demands on intellectual stimulation, which matters more to you than actual achievements. Your ideas are original and progressive. A born leader, you can give instructions off the top of your head, and you give good advice which you expect other people to follow. You yourself follow your impulses rather than your good sense. You can be headstrong and unreasonable – compromise is not for you. Headaches may be the effect of suppressed anger.

Mercury in Taurus is steady and realistic, thorough and thoughtful, but also somewhat inert. You're not one to jump to conclusions. You hold on to your well-considered opinions, which usually follow convention and prevailing prejudice. Money is rarely missing – in fact, material assets could take up far too much of your time and attention. You're sympathetic and affectionate and like the company of the opposite sex. You may marry someone with money and/or status. Mercury in this position can give a beautiful voice.

Mercury in Gemini is intelligent and quick-witted, but your insight and knowledge are superficial, although extending over a wide range. You usually give the impression of being better informed than you really are. You talk well and profusely and don't let feelings interfere with your logic. Your perception, in fact, often makes you crass. Journalism is your field – you have an ability to grasp a situation immediately. You have a flair for languages and a good sense of humour but can be nervous.

Mercury in Cancer is imaginative and receptive but also passive. You have an excellent retentive memory and take an interest in history. You like to make a good impression on other people – even at the expense of honesty. The suffering and pain of others affect you deeply; your sympathy and consideration often make people confide in you; sensing, perhaps, your talent for empathy and deep psychological understanding. Where your own affairs are concerned, you worry unnecessarily and may develop phobias. Try to overcome narrow-minded and capricious tendencies. Your sense of rhythm is highly developed.

Mercury in Leo loves other people and attempts, with the best of intentions, to guide and control their lives. It's a suitable position for teachers. You're creative, particularly with children and in entertainment. Your own conviction and self-confidence will help you go far. Achievements are consider-

134

able, and the world usually benefits somehow from your advice and experience. Try to resist the temptation to boast and bully others and check your prejudiced dogmatic attitude. Pride and self-importance could seriously impair your mental development.

Mercury in Virgo is efficient and professional – you're intelligent, rational and analytical, but try to be less sceptical, critical and inhuman. You learn easily and are well suited for research, as long as you don't allow the details to cloud the main issue. You have remarkable powers of observation and find it easy to formulate ideas in writing. You think out solutions to irksome problems and have good powers of persuasion. One thing that irritates you more than anything else is stupidity.

Mercury in Libra is well balanced and diplomatic, with excellent judgement. You're good at negotiating but less able when it comes to making decisions and applying them in practice. You work best together with a partner who is prepared to take the lion's share of responsibility and decisions. Manual work is not your cup ot tea – with the possible exception of arts and crafts. Your occupation should be aesthetically appealing. You're frivolous and enjoy social life. You're also intelligent, sensible and capable but your will is weak. Your spouse may be inferior to you.

Mercury in Scorpio is acute and perceptive and excels at making pointed remarks. You look through everything and everyone and have a very special skill of putting your finger right on the spot of a problem and getting to the bottom of it. Very little escapes your notice, and with your suspicion and intuition you can rest assured that no one pulls the wool over your eyes. You're sly and cunning, and your lust for revenge could assume frightening dimensions. As an enemy you're cruel and ruthless, perhaps even sadistic. This, combined with courage and endurance, makes you an excellent spy. You retain your calm in a crisis.

Mercury in Sagittarius is vague and indistinct. It is the position

135

of the eternal student, the perpetual undergraduate. You never stop learning things and are unconcerned about the results. On the other hand, you're broad-minded and alert, honest and just. Very likely, you flourish intellectually in your middle age (possibly in literature) after having been fairly mediocre at school. You're kind and sincere but promise more than you can keep. You jump to conclusions which may lead to serious mistakes. Be careful with unrealistic speculation and try not to be tactless.

Mercury in Capricorn is serious and disciplined, sensible and ambitious, but also cold and calculating. You could be a climber, socially or professionally. A talent for mathematics and natural sciences is likely – you're logical and have an excellent memory. But you lack a sense of humour and may harbour grudges. Try not to be too dissatisfied and negative – your pessimism settles as a wet blanket on even the jolliest mind! As a parent or boss you're usually too strict and demanding.

Mercury in Aquarius is future-orientated and socially aware, fascinated by research and science (in particular social sciences and technology). When it comes to judging other people's character, you're both perceptive and sympathetic, at the same time showing a healthy lack of illusions. You rarely become emotionally involved but are loyal and faithful to both friends and partner. You're most at home in a group of some kind and probably belong to some ideological organization. Controversial discussions stimulate you. Your social conscience is more active that most.

Mercury in Pisces is impressionable and easily confused, forgetful and absent-minded. Your imagination is powerful – but you may get carried away. You easily identify with other people's feelings – you have great powers of both empathy and imitation. Your self-knowledge is admirable, because you remember feelings well and often reflect on childhood experiences. Responsibility does not appeal to you, but you enjoy working for institutions, helping those worse off. Your resistance against stress is low and you need support not to collapse in a crisis. In a healthy, encouraging environment, your artistic talent, a good heart and a sense of humour will flourish.

Planets in different signs: *Venus*

Venus in Aries is ardent, fiery and attractive, seldom satisfied with one partner. At first you're likely to shower gifts and affection over the loved one, but you will soon become selfish and restless, perhaps even cruel and ruthless. You often marry on the spur of the moment and live to regret it. Your problem is a need for security coupled with a craving for freedom. You expect co-operation – but only on your terms! Emotionally, you're superficial rather than hard. It's fairly easy to appeal to your sympathy, and you may be fooled by appearances.

Venus in Taurus is constant. You mature late sexually, but when the time has come, you set your heart on a certain person whom you subsequently win over and then hold on to for the rest of your life. You are sensual and physically inclined and quite attractive. Unfortunately you have a tendency to regard your partner as a possession and you could well be jealous. You enjoy eating and are probably a good cook – something which may lead to a weight problem. At home you surround yourself with luxury and comfort, and you collect beautiful possessions. You're kind and considerate, affable and gracious.

Venus in Gemini is volatile and fickle. Emotional ties are treated lightly; you're a great flirt and won't marry too early. You may well understand love intellectually, but it takes a lot before you experience it heart and soul. Your cheerful, easygoing nature attracts a lot of admirers, and you may well keep several affairs going simultaneously. Several marriages are likely. You have no difficulty in discussing your feelings but could easily talk romantic situations to pieces.

Venus in Cancer is warm and protective, a nice position, provided the love doesn't smother the partner. You're a superb cook and prefer staying at home, where you create a cosy, comfortable nest for you and your loved ones. Try not to worry so much about those you love or fuss over them like a mother hen. You're romantic and weak when it comes to love, and extremely vulnerable – perhaps you're safest with people who have had bad experiences in the past and therefore appreciate your best traits. You soon recover from disappointments, but that's no excuse for scaring the partner off with emotional scenes.

Venus in Leo is affectionate and popular, with a tendency to place the loved one on a pedestal, showering money and love over him/her. In return you expect your partner to submit to your domination. If necessary you will, however, accept a noble self-sacrifice. Usually you enjoy life and appreciate pleasure, children and the arts. You're bound to be glamorous, just like your partner. Being admired and impressing others is important to you. You could benefit through children or inheritance.

Venus in Virgo is cool and practical – not an ideal position. You analyse and criticize first your own feelings and then those of your partner, seeing his/her insignificant weaknesses as major faults. This hardly induces romance! You should have someone who appreciates your care and attention; if this is impossible on a personal level, you could choose a job where your consideration and sense of duty will be valued. You're tidy and refined. Marriage will bring money and security – you, of course, would never consider any other alternative.

Venus in Libra is sensual and generous – a strong position. Your greatest happiness is found in a harmonious relationship with another person. The act of love is an important ritual, and you worship your partner. Your gentle, sensitive and easy-going nature usually ensures that your love is returned. Socially, you present a charming façade – but give very little of yourself. Beauty and the arts appeal to you, and you enjoy working in these fields. Harmonious surroundings are a necessity – you're soon broken down by sordid or ugly conditions.

Venus in Scorpio is sexy, passionate and sexually demanding. You're intense and emotional, with strong repressed feelings, and can be violently possessive and jealous. Try not to dominate your partner sexually; quarrels and aggression on your part can reduce him/her to a nervous wreck. Safeguard your morals – you're more sensitive to temptation than most. Venereal disease and a drink problem are your worst hazards. In favourable cases, you're perceptive and efficient, generous and prepared to share everything with your partner.

Venus in Sagittarius loves its freedom and prefers bachelor life. You give the impression of being more passionate than you really are. Sometimes your friends get more love and loyalty than your sex partner; the type of relationship that survives involves a high degree of companionship and personal independence. If your chart has planets in Scorpio, you will experience an inner conflict between possessing and being free. You love the outdoors and travelling. Relationships with foreigners seem to bring out your warmest feelings, perhaps because a certain distance is enforced due to cultural differences?

Venus in Capricorn is cold and conventional, in extreme cases suffering from emotional blockages. Fear of being rejected or deceived may induce you to deny love completely and give money and status a deputizing rôle. Marriage of convenience is common. You mature late sexually – the later you marry, the better the prospects. Marriage may be to a person of considerable age difference. Your serious, responsible nature in due course attracts wealth and respect. Your integrity is above reproach, but you never forget a slight.

Venus in Aquarius is detached but shows a true humanitarian. In close relationships you insist on retaining your independence. You're not particularly warm or demonstrative, but strange and bizarre love affairs seem inevitable. You either marry young, get divorced and remarry later, or remain single for some time. You're a very good judge of character and extremely tolerant regarding other people's weaknesses.

Because of that you have friends in all strata of society. You also have a healthy attitude to money.

Venus in Pisces is well placed and gives a good, warm heart. Kindness is second nature to you, and you direct it towards mankind as a whole, without expecting anything in return. Perhaps you should try just a little discrimination, to stop unworthy people taking advantage of you? You have a lot to offer – but give it to those who deserve and appreciate it! When in love, you're devoted, although your partner may be inferior and disappointing. You can be inspired and artistic but tend to lack ambition and motivation. You're often dependent on others, especially where finances are concerned.

Planets in different signs: *Mars*

Mars in Aries is forceful and energetic but not always sensible. Rashness could lead to accidents, particularly cuts and burns. Most of the time you do exactly what you want, and in sport and other vigorous activities you often end up victorious. You have a strong sex drive which you selfishly seek to gratify – if this fails, you become aggressive. Quarrels don't deter you – with your hot-blooded temperament you enjoy clearing the air now and then. Your rages can be violent.

Mars in Taurus is determined if not obstinate. Your fury is violent, although it takes a lot to arouse it. Your first priority in life is acquisition – including a partner whom you guard jealously. You're sexy and voluptuous with beautiful movements. At work you adhere to rules and instructions and would make a good executive. You climb slowly but steadily. Unfortunately your preoccupation with worldly values means that you miss out on satisfaction in less material spheres.

Mars in Gemini is vivacious and inventive. You're dexterous but find it hard to concentrate – you like to talk, read or write but prefer to vary your interests. Your intelligence is above average, and your achievements are likely to be intellectual. You often get involved in a number of different things at the same time and may not conclude any of them. You're nervous and will soon get harassed and irritable. You may lie and exaggerate and make fun of other people.

Mars in Cancer is creative and artistic, although not always duly appreciated. Your greatest problem is your variable moods – you're quick to take offense and soon become peevish, irritable and crabby. Your childhood may have been unsettled and you probably still feel insecure. The home is of great importance. Your intuition provides special insight and your sense of humour is a help in most situations. You have an unusual ability to perceive historical perspectives. Your self-confidence improves with work in an official capacity.

Mars in Leo is ambitious and determined. You're a forceful, magnanimous person – affectionate, generous and sociable. Your heart rules and you have great confidence in life and yourself. Sometimes you're over-optimistic and set out to do things you have no chance to conclude, but most of your grandiose schemes meet with support and admiration. One problem is a tendency physically to advance too fast. You can also be arrogant and domineering.

Mars in Virgo is restrained and puritanical, loyal and stead-fast. You lack warmth and imagination and may be tempted to feign feelings you haven't got if you believe they are expected. But as far as possible you avoid emotionally demanding situations and hide the fact that you're lonely and insecure. At work you're practical, diligent and inventive, but you prefer to work under someone else, since too much responsibility tends to worry you. Research and science suit your painstaking sense of detail. You plan everything care-fully – including your economy.

Mars in Libra is fair, with good judgement. Nothing makes you more incensed than social injustice. With your wise and well-balanced mind, you could be useful to the world, and you're often found in official positions. Your assets include amiability and good powers of persuasion. Your energy, like your sex drive, fluctuates. You fall in love easily (too easily?) and may marry too early and divorce after quarrels and disappointments have taken their toll. Your life and career take colour from your partner; you can't separate his/her needs from your own. You enjoy physical pleasures, good food and drink, the arts and good conversation.

Mars in Scorpio is dignified and reserved. You possess an enormous amount of dammed-up energy which screams for an outlet. The channel you usually choose for it is sex. Your desires and passions are extremely strong. If sexual conquests are not enough to satisfy you, you may seize upon other means to gain power over others: emotions, cunning, cruelty, violence, aggression, brutality. Once you've set your aim, you will strive towards it, regardless of the expense. In order to avoid destructivity, which in the long run will harm yourself as well as others, you should try to externalize your strong emotional and physical needs and find a spiritual outlet for your sharp, penetrating intellect.

Mars in Sagittarius is high-spirited, convivial and humorous, with great moral courage. Your problem is a tendency to over-optimism and exaggeration, and you rarely conclude projects. Your attraction to adventure, freedom and travel doesn't make you an ideal marriage partner. Your intellect is swift and active – you question a lot of things but don't usually bother to find out the answers. You're athletic and fond of outdoor life, but don't be reckless in sport! Your energy is always on the way up or down, never static.

Mars in Capricorn is constructive – the best place for Mars. You apply your energy sensibly to achieve healthy objectives. A successful career is your main aim in life. You're patient, not to say indefatigable. Waste and incompetence are things you can't stand. As an executive you flourish – both superiors and inferiors share your own belief in your ability. You expect obedience and respect and can be strict and demanding. Usually your greatest success comes late in life, but you can have some early achievements, e.g. in sport.

Mars in Aquarius is impulsive but purposeful. Your arguments for social reform are difficult to counter, and you often devote yourself to bold pioneering pursuits in the interest of the public. Although you're happiest in a group situation, you will soon end up the obvious leader of every team you join. Large humanitarian organizations benefit greatly from your leadership. Your ideas could lead to considerable social improvement, but don't be too eccentric and miss your target. Freedom appeals to you more than security, and you don't need marriage to survive.

Mars in Pisces is unworldly. Life can expose you to practical demands and difficulties that you're unable to cope with. An artistic profession (perhaps dancing or acting) may prove the shield you need to avoid a direct confrontation with harsh realities. Another solution is to represent other people in a deputizing capacity. You easily become confused or depressed in your search for a fulfilment of a kind which is not quite of this world. Disappointment in life and other people may drive you to seek comfort in sex, alcohol or drugs.

Planets in different signs: *Jupiter*

Jupiter in Aries has grandiose aspirations. Your initiative can achieve a lot, as long as you're not bogged down by detail and other trivialities. Your courage – rash and foolhardy at times – could make you famous, but that is no excuse for despising more cautious creatures. You love sport, provided you can take active part in it and, preferably, win. You're purposeful and self-sufficient. Marriage may bring money and status. Energy, enthusiasm and luck take you far.

Jupiter in Taurus likes a luxurious, comfortable home. You strive hard to reach the material standard you require. Anything to do with property, agriculture and finance will be successful. You're generous, warm-hearted and affectionate. You collect things that are beautiful – and valuable! Try to overcome a tendency to over-indulgence in all the good things in life – including sex! You're reliable, with good judgement, and usually follow prevailing ethical norms. You may have a beautiful singing voice.

143

Jupiter in Gemini has lofty ideas. You talk well and can be both entertaining and persuasive. Listening and receiving impressions is more difficult for you. Your interests are academic but too widely dispersed to give a deeper knowledge in any one subject. You're clever but impractical. Your greatest success will come in a job where your quick tongue and glibness are an asset. A good musical ear is likely. Friends come and go in your life. You may be unable to commit yourself to people or plans. Don't be indiscreet.

Jupiter in Cancer is a favourable position. You're kind, generous, warm and protective, with a special talent for understanding other people's problems, perhaps on a political level. You're happiest in your own comfortable home. Antiques should appeal to you. You have a good business sense and sound financial judgement, although you also like to spend your money. Your sense of inner security emanates from a happy childhood and a good relationship with your mother. You rely on authorities. Be moderate with food, drink and sex.

Jupiter in Leo is magnanimous, affectionate and just, with enormous ambitions. You love splendour, drama and glamour. Popularity and fame are one possibility – you will no doubt reach an elevated position, in society, supported by the authorities. Your judgement in business is sound, and investments prove lucky. But don't let yourself develop into a pompous social climber. You have good prospects for becoming self-satisfied and boastful.

Jupiter in Virgo is rational and efficient but can also become very limited, narrow-minded, sceptical and cynical. A good business sense is your main asset. Your emotional life may have been left behind. You lack spontaneity and often feel stiff and formal in company. Social life does not appeal to you much – you're over-critical towards others and do not make friends easily. Research and science are your field, although you may let details cloud the main issue. Your marriage partner is probably socially or intellectually inferior. Marriage could limit your personal development.

Jupiter in Libra is broad-minded and refined. You have a good talent to assist others, although your own personal affairs may cause problems: you're wasteful and careless with money. Love could bring luck, and a happy marriage is likely. You're concerned about making a good impression on others and are probably hospitable. Try to overcome your own vanity and don't over-indulge in food and drink. You should have a scientific, artistic or academic profession; perhaps the law is your best choice, because you attach great value to justice.

Jupiter in Scorpio is shrewd and strong-willed. Your power and your strategies are hard to resist. In business your judgement is good and you're not harassed in a crisis. Excess energy is best released through sex. You're a master at hiding your emotions – even to yourself! Make sure you don't repeat your mistakes! Power holds special appeal to you, and with it you could achieve much for the benefit of society, possibly on government level. But don't abuse it! You could also be a skilful sleuth, surgeon or psychiatrist.

Jupiter in Sagittarius is lucky. Somehow you attract all the things you require in life, and you have a sixth sense protecting you from deceitful people and dangerous situations. Studies and literature appeal to you, and you're a generous host or hostess. Your circle includes many different types of people, whom you select for their inner qualities, and you love animals, horses in particular – they can also bring luck. You're interested in sports and the outdoors. Residence abroad is not unlikely. You're optimistic, tolerant and humorous. But don't gamble too much and don't be wasteful, boastful, careless or exaggerated.

Jupiter in Capricorn is responsible. Success follows on hard, determined efforts. You're thorough, conventional and orthodox – perhaps also self-righteous, stiff, stingy and contained. You have good powers of concentration and a splendid business sense – no wonder you go far! But an idealistic outlook on life would increase the depth of your achievements. You're as cautious as you are enthusiastic – but the two don't conflict in your case – they serve each other, with very good results! You are obviously pre-destined for a position in authority.

Jupiter in Aquarius is idealistic and socially aware. You try out new methods to assist mankind – a perfect position for social, scientific or humanitarian achievements. You're good at administration, an expert at handling both people and situations. Your ambitions are honourable and detached from the materialistic aspects, your methods are original and your inventive mind usually appeals to the public. Your many different friends often come to your assistance. But be prepared for sudden changes in your life.

Jupiter in Pisces is pleasant: benevolence is coupled with genuine sympathy. You're sensitive rather than intellectual and extremely idealistic. High spirits, a sense of humour and an easy-going attitude contribute to your popularity. You're kind and helpful to everybody and don't mind sacrificing your own interests to assist those worse off. But don't let unscrupulous people take advantage of you. You may become restless and indecisive and flit from one place to another. Periodically you need to isolate yourself preferably in the country. Music also helps restore your equilibrium.

Planets in different signs: *Saturn*

Saturn in Aries could be limiting. Strength and weakness alternate due to psychological problems. In childhood, life was most difficult: you probably had a difficult domineering father: you're ambitious and persevering, and your pioneering spirit is well suited to official projects, but you must learn a few lessons in co-operation. You could become frustrated and headstrong, and your temper flares up at regulᴗr intervals. Marriage could prove unlucky. Your partner wants you as a shield, and you refuse to be one. You may suffer from severe headaches, poor health or a physical handicap.

Saturn in Taurus is patient and cautious. Your main driving force is your practical, methodical mind, and the stumbling-block your emotions which are repressed and controlled to the extent that you can't express them even when you want to. Material things cause you a lot of anxiety, and if you ever have a nervous breakdown, it's probably due to financial brooding. You're kind and considerate and find your greatest happiness through beautiful scenery, art and music. Try not to be mean or miserly!

Saturn in Gemini gives an intellectual or scientific talent. Your good powers of observation make you a good teacher or author. You could study several subjects simultaneously and have a serious and profound side coupled with a good sense of humour. Your story-telling could be extremely amusing. You're a late developer – the older you get, the better you express yourself, and the more lovable you become. Unfortunate circumstances in childhood may have made you hard or bitter, but try to forget and look forward instead!

Saturn in Cancer craves more security than others because of a constant feeling of inadequacy. You can be very insecure, moody and self-centred and given to self-pity, melancholy and lack of self-respect. You're limited by psychological problems stemming from childhood; you probably had a strict, domineering mother. The consequence of this is an inability to act constructively and independently and an ensuing need constantly to justify your existence. The rôle of a bitter, self-sacrificing martyr is near at hand. You attach excessive significance to family relations.

Saturn in Leo is disciplined and strict. You probably feel that life is asking a lot of you. This, by all means, brings you worldly achievement – but unfortunately at the expense of your private life. You find it hard to enjoy yourself in a light-hearted way – your joy comes through the eminence and respect you enjoy. In the same way you're inhibited when it comes to expressing feelings and warmth. As a compensation you work even harder, not realizing that such self-centred ambition only serves further to increase your isolation. Remember that power and authority are no substitute for personal happiness.

Saturn in Virgo is methodical, conscientious, dutiful, tidy and diligent. You have high demands on both yourself and others: work to you is a purpose in itself. You are well suited to research projects. Unfortunately, every occasion in life gives you something to worry about, and you're often depressed. Your manners are reserved and considerate. You're thrifty and likely to have a stable economy. Your ever-critical, negative attitude makes you difficult to live with. You may have had problems, perhaps bad health, in childhood.

Saturn in Libra is a favourable position. You find it easy to express love and affection and enjoy your relations with other people, perhaps through some kind of creative or artistic activity. You're moderate, placid and impartial, with good judgement. Problems could be brought on by partnerships or marriage, which is likely to show a certain age difference. You're intelligent and scientifically endowed but could be impractical. If success comes early in life, you may not keep it forever.

Saturn in Scorpio gives a forceful character with a strong sense of purpose under a pleasant façade. You have a good business sense; you know exactly what you're doing and why. You're reserved and serious and enjoy secretly manipulating others, sometimes without any great scruples. You could be a good spy, detective, surgeon or psychiatrist. Your feelings are deep but repressed, and this together with your strong sex drive could lead to considerable frustration. Woe betide whoever deceives you! Your lust for revenge will sooner or later find an expression. Your own lack of inner security doesn't stop you being selfish or despotic.

Saturn in Sagittarius can achieve plenty, although success may come late in life. You're idealistic and socially aware, philosophical, bold, honest and popular. Your generosity benefits other people – you don't spend a lot on your own person. Usually your word is trustworthy – but safeguard your reputation and keep away from law courts! You tend to take wild chances which undermine your basic security.

Saturn in Capricorn enjoys discipline and responsibility. You're very ambitious and may well sacrifice your private life for worldly success. You could be selfish, hard and pessimistic – stingy towards yourself as well as others. People like you are often snobs or social climbers – power and authority appeal to you. At heart you're petrified of being hurt or ridiculed; your unfeeling nature is not very successful in love, and you will either decide not to marry at all or marry for social reasons. Your private life could lead to brooding and depression, while the world sees you as a brightly shining star.

Saturn in Aquarius is well placed. Purpose in life and humanitarian ideals are given top priority. You learn easily and are well suited to scientific work. Your attitude to other people is extraverted and responsible. Team work appeals to you most, although you immediately become the leader of the group. Any contact with the public, politics especially, is favourable. Your marriage is unconventional but lasting, because you're a loyal and faithful person. Your opinions could benefit from being slightly less extreme.

Saturn in Pisces provides great assets, such as intuition and imagination, but the position makes you less skilled in wrestling with harsh reality and trivial problems. Unfortunately, you seem to have more than your fair share of this sort of thing – perhaps because you try too hard to evade it. Your best bet is to work assisting other people, preferably in institutions. Any humanitarian purpose in life will protect you from disappointment, which otherwise seems inevitable. Actually, you're your own worst enemy. You let your despondency devour all your willpower.

Planets in different signs: *Uranus*

The position of Uranus in a chart shows a long-term influence which has to be related to the chart as a whole.

Uranus in Aries is original, headstrong and impulsive. Freedom and independence mean a lot to you. Don't be

149

impatient and intolerant to people who are slower and more cautious than yourself!

Uranus in Taurus is immovable, stubborn and strong-willed. You crave security, often in the form of possessions. Artistic talent is one possibility. Jealousy could cause problems in your emotional life.

Uranus in Gemini is inventive and intellectually advanced – literature or science is your field. You could be nervous or eccentric. Your assets include good powers of persuasion, flair for languages and literary talent.

Uranus in Cancer is insecure, moody and passive, but at the same time quite popular. Your environment makes a strong imprint on your mind. Home life is often unsettled. Nervous stomach problems could be a problem.

Uranus in Leo is self-assured, domineering and rebellious. Any creative talent is very original. Your life is exciting – you never know what will happen next! This applies in particular to your stormy love life.

Uranus in Virgo is hypercritical and analytical but at the same time original and full of ideas. Your intellectual energy fluctuates and you find it hard to concentrate. You could be nervous and capricious.

Uranus in Libra is sociable and Bohemian. You attach great significance to justice. Your social life goes up and down, and friends may suddenly turn into enemies. Marriage is entered into without warning and tends to shock others.

Uranus in Scorpio is shrewd, purposeful, unpredictable and explosive. Your life undergoes sudden changes. You have a sharp tongue, and your sexual relationships are bound to be stormy.

Uranus in Sagittarius is changeable, careless and generous.

You're bold and adventurous. Freedom of speech means a lot to you. Your finances could prove a source of worry.

Uranus in Capricorn is capable and ambitious. Your business sense is good. You work very hard, usually in an executive position, but try not to be too domineering and tyrannical.

Uranus in Aquarius is original, unconventional and popular. You like to work for the benefit of mankind. Your friends may be eccentric or anti-social. Political opinions can be fanatical.

Uranus in Pisces is sympathetic and self-sacrificing. But your expectations in life are unrealistic and disappointments are inevitable. You frequently change your residence.

Planets in different signs: *Neptune*

The position of Neptune in a chart shows a generation influence which has to be related to the chart as a whole.

Neptune in Leo is well placed, creative and glamorous. This generation gave us Hollywood and the film industry. You often have an uplifting effect on the world and a good influence on children. But your love life may be unsatisfactory.

Neptune in Virgo is rather cool but sets high standards and criticizes social conditions. You're shy and retiring and prefer to work behind the scenes. Your generation reformed the educational system.

Neptune in Libra is idealistic but not very effective. You identify strongly with your own generation, which created the concepts of hippies and flower-power in the sixties. Your manners are gentle and pleasant.

Neptune in Scorpio is destructive and likes to shock. This is the punk generation. You hate affectation and hypocrisy and are scrupulously honest to yourself.

Neptune in Sagittarius is idealistic and future-orientated. You

151

have a philosophical outlook on life which elevates and improves prevailing conditions. You take an interest in higher education and outdoor life.

Neptune in Capricorn is practical and materialistic. You will probably concentrate on methods to make better use of the world's resources. Your private life may be less satisfactory.

Planets in different signs: *Pluto*

The position of Pluto in a chart shows a trend spanning over generations and has to be related to the chart as a whole. The planet was discovered as late as 1930, and we can only speculate on its different manifestations. Usually its effect reaches out to the masses.

Pluto in Cancer (1914–38) challenged and destroyed the prevailing family pattern. Women's emancipation started with these generations, and society became more competitive.

Pluto in Leo (1938–57) introduced sexual liberation. Great efforts are made by these generations to improve the conditions of the masses. Another side of its influence is international terrorism.

Pluto in Virgo (1957–71) gave us a generation which may well devote itself to ecology, at the same time introducing new work methods with the aid of new technology.

Pluto in Libra (1971–83) should have an effect on improved justice and equality on an international scale, or at least make an honest attempt in that direction. If nothing else, it holds a promise of improved political relations.

Pluto in Scorpio (1983–96) is a powerful position and we can only imagine its effect on the world. Some kind of social and political transformation seems inevitable. Let's hope it's for the better!

Planets in different houses: *The Sun*

Sun in House I	gives a self-centred, egotistical nature. You judge all things from your own personal perspective. Are you too self-righteous?
Sun in House II	gives a materialistic nature, craving constantly increasing resources. You probably have a high income – but do you share it with anyone?
Sun in House III	gives a person in constant pursuit of new impressions. You express yourself well verbally – but what about your powers of concentration?
Sun in House IV	gives a happy home life but insecurity outside the home. Remember that the whole wonderful world is waiting for you out there. Are you intolerant to outsiders?
Sun in House V	gives joy, creative talent and fondness for pleasures. You get on well with children – but do you dominate others too much?
Sun in House VI	gives happiness at work and good powers of organization. Your health is important – perhaps too important – to you.
Sun in House VII	gives a happy marriage and successful partnerships. You're best suited for being the dominant partner.
Sun in House VIII	gives chances of inheritance and work in banking, insurance or industry. You have a healthy attitude towards death. But do you force your will onto others?
Sun in House IX	gives opportunities for higher education and long-distance travel. You're philosophical and have a

153

	flair for languages. Your integrity should be above reproach.
Sun in House X	gives a successful career and a responsible, dutiful character. But does your private life suffer?
Sun in House XI	gives an inclination for humanitarian work. You have many friends and usually achieve your objectives. But are you eccentric?
Sun in House XII	gives a risk of isolation, voluntary or not. You have great abilities to assist others. But do you have a tendency to escapism?

Planets in different houses: *The Moon*

Moon in House I	gives a receptive, sensitive mind. A strong relationship with your mother should have given you a sense of inner security. But are you excessively moody?
Moon in House II	gives a high income and security through material things. You're happy to save and invest. But do you over-estimate the value of possessions?
Moon in House III	gives a constant stream of new impulses and ideas. You find it easy to express thoughts and impressions. But do you change your mind too often?
Moon in House IV	gives a happy home life. You're very protective. But are you too dependent on your family?
Moon in House V	gives success in creative work. You enjoy leading and encouraging children. But do you let them develop independently?
Moon in House VI	gives a clean, tidy home. You may have had delicate health in child-

	hood. Is cleanliness an obsession?
Moon in House VII	gives importance to relations with women. You find your security through marriage. Are you overly dependent on your partner?
Moon in House VIII	gives opportunities in banking, insurance or industry. Sex is important to you, and control of other people's emotions. Do your own strong feelings occasionally run away with you?
Moon in House IX	gives a talent for academic pursuits and a flair for languages and literature. You may well take up residence abroad.
Moon in House X	gives a successful career, possibly fame. You take life and yourself seriously. Do you neglect your private life?
Moon in House XI	gives involvement in ideological or humanitarian pursuits. You're happiest in the company of friends or people who share your opinions. Are you dogmatic?
Moon in House XII	gives introversion and tendencies to escapism. If the psychological conditions are favourable, intuition and inspiration will flourish. Are you a hermit?

Planets in different houses: *Mercury*

Mercury in House I	gives an alert but self-centred mind. You prefer to have your own way. Are you too headstrong?
Mercury in House II	gives material success through verbal talent. You're an excellent salesman. Original ideas will increase your income – hopefully in a legal way.

155

Mercury in House III	gives a nervous, talkative nature but also above-average intelligence. You're a good teacher if you can concentrate on one subject long enough. Do you tell lies?
Mercury in House IV	gives a vivid exchange of thoughts and ideas in the home. You're interested in history and like to study at home. Are you capricious?
Mercury in House V	gives a creative mind. You enjoy fun and games that challenge the intellect. Children have much to offer you. Do you respect other people's ideas?
Mercury in House VI	gives a specialized, skilled occupation. You're diligent and meticulous at work but have a tendency to worry. Have you ever had nervous stomach trouble?
Mercury in House VII	gives intellectually stimulating relations to other people. If your partner expects to keep you, he must live up to your mental standards. Are you fickle?
Mercury in House VIII	gives a mental strength and an attraction to the occults, possibly a preoccupation with death or life after death. You may work in banking, insurance or industry.
Mercury in House IX	gives an interest in higher education, a flair for languages and literary talent. Your outlook on life is philosophical. Are you too quick off the mark?
Mercury in House X	gives chances of solid training and a successful career – or the opposite, unhappiness and frustration at work. The communications industry may appeal to you.
Mercury in House XI	gives an intense social life and active

| | participation in societies and organizations. You have high ideals – but are you too theoretical? |
| Mercury in House XII | gives a tendency to secrecy and a vivid imagination which should be given an external expression. Do you find it hard to voice your opinion? |

Planets in different houses: *Venus*

Venus in House I	gives an attractive appearance. You attach great significance to love and pleasure and probably had a happy childhood. Are you lazy and spoilt by life?
Venus in House II	gives a great appreciation of beautiful things. You are, or will soon be, wealthy, possibly through work in the arts.
Venus in House III	gives an interest in aesthetically appealing subjects. You're witty and entertaining socially.
Venus in House IV	gives a beautiful home. You would make a good interior designer. Can you afford all the money you spend on your home?
Venus in House V	gives creative talent and love for the arts. You are fond of pleasure and enjoy the company of children.
Venus in House VI	gives a craving for aesthetically appealing working conditions, possibly in beauty care or hairdressing. Love may come through your work.
Venus in House VII	gives gracious manners and popularity, possibly fame. Marriage is of vital importance to you.
Venus in House VIII	gives good chances of inheritance. Sexual relations are important and

157

highly satisfactory, although you can go through periods of enforced celibacy.

Venus in House IX   gives success in higher education and happiness in an academic environment. Relations with foreigners are fortunate – you may even marry one.

Venus in House X   gives happiness and success at work. You have good relationships with parents and people in authority.

Venus in House XI   gives success in societies and organizations. You are kind, sympathetic and sociable and have many friends.

Venus in House XII   gives a propensity for secret love affairs and a need for isolation. You are kind and sensitive. Do you daydream about love?

Planets in different houses: *Mars*

Mars in House I   gives enthusiasm, energy and aggression. You over-estimate your strength. Are you impatient?

Mars in House II   gives a high income. But you spend the money as soon as you earn it.

Mars in House III   gives an astute mind. You don't mind challenging people with your opinions. Are you too self-assertive?

Mars in House IV   gives dedication in improving the home and a tendency to quarrel with the family.

Mars in House V   gives an active love life. Work with children stimulates you and could bring out your great creative talent.

Mars in House VI   gives high standards for yourself and others in work situations. You expect everyone to work as hard as

	you. Do you neglect your health?
Mars in House VII	gives an active marital life. Your partner could be a source of dis- appointment. Do you quarrel excessively?
Mars in House VIII	gives a strong sex drive. You would be a good surgeon, detective, accountant or con-man.
Mars in House IX	gives a liking for travel and adventure. You could be an active athlete. With motivation, you could do well in higher education.
Mars in House X	gives a lot of hard work. You're so ambitious that you may become ruthless in your struggle to reach the top.
Mars in House XI	gives a steady stream of friends and acquaintances moving through your life. You devote yourself wholeheartedly to your objectives in life.
Mars in House XII	gives a likelihood for contact with institutions. You're very self-contained and could become self-destructive.

Planets in different houses: *Jupiter*

Jupiter in House I	gives optimism and success in life. You're broad-minded, benevolent and tolerant. But try not to over-indulge. Do you have a weight problem?
Jupiter in House II	gives appreciation of material assets. You make plenty of money without much effort. But are you too extravagant?
Jupiter in House III	gives success in school life. You find it easy to enthuse and persuade others. You could go far in the communications industry.

Jupiter in House IV	gives a happy home life and good relations with parents and your own children. You're a hospitable, generous host.
Jupiter in House V	gives appreciation of pleasure and creative work. You could be lucky in speculation. But does the gambling instinct take over at times?
Jupiter in House VI	gives joy and satisfaction at work and a good income. Any ill health has good prospects of recovery, but watch your liver.
Jupiter in House VII	gives good prospects for marriage and partnership, which could prove lucrative. But don't take them for granted. Are you occasionally unfaithful?
Jupiter in House VIII	gives good chances of inheritance and a healthy attitude to death. Your greatest success will come in banking, insurance, industry or related fields.
Jupiter in House IX	gives success in academic or literary professions. You have a flair for languages and like travelling abroad.
Jupiter in House X	gives great professional achievements and a high income. You're well suited for a public career – but it may be at the expense of your home life.
Jupiter in House XI	gives progress in connection with ideological or humanitarian organizations. Friends are very lucky for you.
Jupiter in House XII	gives good prospects of productive inspired work. Success could come through art, dance, poetry or a

medical profession. Any humanitarian work gives great satisfaction.

Planets in different houses: *Saturn*

Saturn in House I	gives limitation. You're probably hampered by physical or mental circumstances. You may have been delicate as a child or orphaned early.
Saturn in House II	gives hard work for every penny you earn. But in due course you accumulate wealth. Are you mean?
Saturn in House III	gives deficient early education. Perhaps you had to assume extra responsibility as a child – e.g. for younger brothers and sisters. Do you have difficulty in expressing yourself lightly?
Saturn in House IV	gives unfortunate conditions at home, physically or mentally. Did you have all you needed as a child? Were your parents harsh and unsympathetic?
Saturn in House V	gives problems with children – you may have them late in life or not at all. Your father was probably strict. Do you ever let your hair down and just enjoy yourself?
Saturn in House VI	gives enforced duties and little freedom at work. But you don't complain. Ailments could linger – skin and gall bladder are prone to infection.
Saturn in House VII	gives marriage late in life and/or marriage with a large age gap. You will probably have to take responsibility for both of you.
Saturn in House VIII	gives responsibility for other people's assets. Your sex life rarely

	flourishes. Is it because you're too inhibited and repressed?
Saturn in House IX	gives a profound, serious philosophical outlook on life. You may be unlucky in contact with foreign countries or travelling.
Saturn in House X	gives a lonely, responsible position. You're ambitious and disciplined. But have you forgotten that there are other values in life, which can be quite pleasant?
Saturn in House XI	gives serious ideals and objectives. You prefer the company of older people. Do you let the end justify the means?
Saturn in House XII	gives loneliness and brooding. You find it difficult to share pain and grief. Do you ever accept the support of others?

Planets in different houses: *Uranus*

Uranus in House I	gives an original, forthright, outspoken nature, possibly eccentric or perverted. You abhor any kind of personal restriction.
Uranus in House II	gives an unsettled economy, with sudden turns for the better or worse. Try to think of unusual ways to make money.
Uranus in House III	gives an unsettled early education. You have a way of expressing yourself that is vivacious and original.
Uranus in House IV	gives unsettled home conditions and fights in the family. Domestic peace is seldom within reach.
Uranus in House V	gives an exciting, unpredictable love life with original inclinations. Your children are unusual and creative.

Uranus in House VI	gives unusual and varying working conditions in some interesting field. Are your nerves weak?
Uranus in House VII	gives an unconventional marriage to an original partner who isn't the easiest person to live with.
Uranus in House VIII	gives an unconventional sex life with many different, fascinating partners. Your economical circumstances are unsettled and risky.
Uranus in House IX	gives exciting adventures abroad and studies of original subjects.
Uranus in House X	gives a changeable career, possibly in films or television. You can't bear routine work for long.
Uranus in House XI	gives unusual objectives and membership in extreme organizations. You have many different eccentric friends.
Uranus in House XII	gives a secret attraction to unusual, possibly tabooed subjects. You may have deep-seated subconscious conflicts.

Planets in different houses: *Neptune*

Neptune in House I	gives a magnetic attraction but a weak, easily led character. Do you have a tendency to escapism?
Neptune in House II	gives financial confusion. Art and other aesthetic values can be either a source of income or a temptation to extravagance. Are you gullible?
Neptune in House III	gives a vivid imagination. You express yourself in a charming, lyrical fashion. But do you always adhere to fact?
Neptune in House IV	gives a cosy but untidy home. There could be misunderstandings in the family. Are you overly dependent on a parent?

163

Neptune in House V	gives high ideals in love and happiness through children and/or creative pursuits. You're attracted to the film world and theatre.
Neptune in House VI	gives an aversion to routine work. You prefer to work with ideological motives. Have you ever been food-poisoned?
Neptune in House VII	gives a romantic marriage to an idealistic partner. But everyday trivialities may prove a threat to your happiness.
Neptune in House VIII	gives confusion over finances, in-heritance, taxes and related areas. All these things should be left in the hands of professional counsellors.
Neptune in House IX	gives strong inspiration and idealism. You could have a latent interest in literature, philosophy or religion. This should be developed further.
Neptune in House X	gives ambition with strong idealistic overtones. You're likely to end up in a powerful position where you can achieve a lot. But watch a risk of scandal.
Neptune in House XI	gives ideological conviction and noble objectives. Your friends usually have good intentions and can be very helpful.
Neptune in House XII	gives introversion and escapism. You could have enormous reserves of inspiration and talent which should be fully developed. Are you self-destructive?

Planets in different houses: *Pluto*

Pluto in House I	gives a constant identity crisis. You have a dynamic character and are

undaunted by new beginnings. But do you oppress others?

Pluto in House II gives a good business sense and a dynamic economy. You constantly crave new possessions to replace the old. Do not expect any financial trend to last for ever!

Pluto in House III gives an explosive temper. You're lucid and perceptive but may force your opinions on to others.

Pluto in House IV gives a dominant rôle in the home and a changeable home life.

Pluto in House V gives an intense love life. You suddenly take up creative pursuits. Do you dominate your children?

Pluto in House VI gives tremendous endurance at work. You carry out all your projects, but your health may suffer in the process.

Pluto in House VII gives a dynamic marriage, where either you or your partner indulge in manipulating and dominating the other.

Pluto in House VIII gives craving for power and a good business sense which can easily become self-gratifying. Do you like to experiment sexually?

Pluto in House IX gives good prospects for an advanced scientific or academic career, possibly at odds with prevailing conditions. Foreign contacts stimulate you.

Pluto in House X gives power or attraction to power. You may envy people in authority and challenge them. You more than anyone else should keep away from all kinds of drugs.

Pluto in House XI gives involvement in social issues and scientific or humanitarian work. But are your reforms aimed at tearing down rather than building up?

Pluto in House XII   gives a powerful subconscious which may manifest itself in unmotivated guilty feelings. Do you have self-destructive tendencies?

4 Interpreting the aspects

Now the turn has come to the aspects, which is often regarded as the most fascinating and unpredictable part of the interpretation. Using the information on your data card, read the interpretation of each aspect among the interpretations listed on pp. 169–189.

Where conjunctions are concerned, the interpretation depends on the planets involved. The basis of the interpretation is shown by the diagram in Figure 16. You'll see that certain planets in conjunction become soft in their joint effect, whereas some are neutral and others hard. In the interpretations listed, a soft conjunction is shown by the symbol ☌ S, a neutral one by ☌ N and a hard one by ☌ H. However, if a neutral conjunction receives soft or hard aspects from other planets, it can be treated as soft or hard respectively.

The interpretations are given as strongly polarized – in

	☽	☿	♀	♂	♃	♄	♅	♆	♇
☉	N	S	S	N	S	H	N	N	N
☽		N	S	H	S	H	H	N	N
☿			S	N	S	N	S	H	N
♀				N	S	H	H	N	N
♂					S	H	H	H	N
♃						N	N	N	N
♄							N	H	H
♅								N	N
♆									N
♇									

S = SOFT
H = HARD
N = NEUTRAL

The diagram shows how each conjunction should be interpreted. (After Robert Hand.)

reality you rarely find this kind of extreme manifestation. The purpose of this is to make them more obvious for you and easier to indentify. Traits expressed by the aspects are often dormant, and only you can tell how much they matter in your personal development. Sometimes they are so deep-seated that nobody except the person himself has any idea that they exist.

No chart is 'bad' or 'good'. It always relates to our own values, which vary from person to person. Aspects often describe a function which is neither bad nor good but simply a reflection of early conditioning. For this reason, aspects tell us a lot about our inner motivations.

To interpret transits, go on to page 190.

Description of natal aspects:

Aspects: *The Sun*

SUN TO MOON ☌ N

Soft aspects bring a happy start in life, good emotional adjustment and free, harmonious development. Usually you find your right place in the world instinctively, and on the whole enjoy life. Relations with mother and family are good, and your home life is happy. With your sincere, responsible and ambitious outlook, success is inevitable, on both personal and professional levels. You're popular and often receive help from others. Marriage prospects are good.

Hard aspects are an indication of poor childhood contact with your mother or between your parents. As a consequence, your ego is weak, and your emotions are likely to be blocked and inhibited. You don't choose your place in life but have it thrust upon you by circumstances; you may inherit your position. You seem to get more than your fair share of frustration and discontent. But there is compensation – you have plenty of energy to invest in creative projects – and your achievements are considerable.

SUN TO MERCURY ☌ S

Mercury is very close to the Sun, and therefore the only major aspect ever to develop between them is the conjunction. This could make you dogmatic and categorical and confine your views to a strictly personal standpoint. At the same time it brings robust health.

Hard aspects between these planets do not exist.

SUN TO VENUS ☌ S

Venus is relatively close to the Sun, and the only aspects to appear between these planets are the conjunction and the two minor aspects called the semi-sextile (30°) and the semi-square (45°).

The *conjunction* brings you all the good things in life; you automatically attract all the love, wealth and support you'll ever need. You're popular, graceful, attractive, refined and affectionate. Others feel at ease in your company. It's interesting to note that this aspect is not particularly successful for marriage. You're so secure and self-sufficient that you see no need to compromise just to protect a relationship. You often end up on your own. Luck comes through art and speculation.

The two minor aspects, when they are exact, often appear in the charts of divorced people, partly due to the progression of the Sun (pp. 82–84). Divorce is most likely at the age of thirty (the semi-sextile) or forty-five (the semi-square).

SUN TO MARS ♂ N

Soft aspects bring a happy, passionate lovelife and robust health. You are active and creative, enterprising and vigorous. You know your own mind and make quick decisions. Your ambition and determination produce tangible results – you're frank and courageous, a born leader. Sports and athletics should be successful. You endure physical pain easily.

Hard aspects give an aggressive, restless, combative nature. Your fellow-man is regarded mainly as a competitor, although you are your own worst enemy. You lack endurance and take great risks – rashness is another problem, and your anger can be roused without a better reason than perhaps hurt pride. On such occasions you will be very destructive, perhaps even fighting, physically. Your sexual appetite is considerable and mainly self-seeking.

SUN TO JUPITER ♂ S

Soft aspects are a great asset in any horoscope – they give a broad-minded, benevolent, tolerant and positive nature which attracts support and success. You're basically lucky – opportunities seem to appear from nowhere, circumstances conspire in your favour and you are generally well endowed. People in authority will assist you. You're honest and magnanimous and usually get what you want out of life. There is always enough money for your needs. Books and intellectual pleasures appeal to you.

Hard aspects indicate over-optimism, waste and neglect with money, careless speculation, possibly gambling. Your judgement is bad and you tend to push your luck, which leads to serious disappointments. Keep away from law-courts at any cost! Over-indulgence can result in bad health, in particular liver ailments. You're a bad judge of character and choose the wrong types of associates. This will prove costly in the long run. Besides, you are boastful and conceited.

SUN TO SATURN ☌ ♄

Soft aspects bring success through hard work, integrity and good organization and are common in self-made people who start with two empty hands. Life becomes easier every year, and you keep the results of your efforts, but early life can be difficult. Perhaps your father was cold, domineering or merely unfortunate. You're constructive and disciplined, sensible and practical. You're likely to end up in a responsible position. You accept your limitations and take full advantage of your assets. Longevity is probable.

Hard aspects indicate serious limitations. Your early life was difficult and your father was demanding and unsympathetic. This has made you selfish, negative and pessimistic. You encourage neither yourself nor anyone else. Emotions are seriously blocked and you feel opposed by authorities and those in power. Your energy level is low and you frequently give in to depression and self-pity. Take advantage of your skills at organization and constructive effort, and don't let your assets go to waste. Great achievements are within reach, if you give yourself a change. Marriage could lead to problems, and you may decide that you're better off on your own.

171

SUN TO URANUS ☌ N

Soft aspects bring willpower and an original, creative mind. Your spirit is dynamic and independent, and you exert a magnetic attraction. You have many strange experiences and friends. Life is never dull in your case, and at times it may change drastically. There is more than a hint of genius here – you could well be famous, perhaps in television, science or technology.

Hard aspects are an indication of an eccentric character with extreme views. You're subject to wild, uncontrollable impulses, which makes you generally unreliable. Convention is not for you, and you refuse to take advice, preferring your own rash actions, which often result in serious mistakes. Even when you occasionally work constructively, you'll ruin the result by some abrupt, erratic change of mind. Love affairs and marriage can prove unlucky – you have a tendency to upset others. You change jobs frequently and provoke changes if they don't come about of their own accord. Hard aspects between the Sun and Uranus make you particularly susceptible to Uranus's transits.

SUN TO NEPTUNE ☌ N

Soft aspects bring imagination and intuition; an inspired, creative, elevated mind. Take advantage of these traits and don't just take them for granted. You're warm and sympathetic and able to understand other people's feelings and motives. You express yourself poetically and may well have a literary talent. Whatever you do is marked by style, elegance and refinement. The sun and the sea appeal to you, as well as animals, horses in particular.

Hard aspects make you a mysterious, confusing creature whom other people find difficult to understand. As a matter of fact, you don't understand yourself very well. At heart you're kind and well-intentioned, but at the same time untidy and unreliable, confused and deceitful. You're also extremely gullible and easily led astray. There's a risk of promiscuity as well as drink and drug abuse. Scandal is another hazard. Try to control your own emotions before they become your undoing. You may suffer from ailments which doctors can't diagnose – probably because they are psychosomatic.

SUN TO PLUTO ☌ N

Soft aspects bring very strong willpower, creative talent, good powers of concentration, perception and endurance. You have an ability to improve your environment and find new methods to solve old problems. Things below the surface will attract your attention. An inner security gives you the courage to regularly abolish that which is old and obsolete in your life and start again from scratch.

Hard aspects make you selfish and ruthless. You may abuse a position of power and be domineering and dictatorial, which is one way of ensuring that all your efforts miss their mark. You have a tendency to over-estimate your own value and strength and take great risks without considering the consequences, which may be dire. There is also a risk of self-destruction.

Aspects: *Moon*

MOON TO MERCURY ☌ N

Soft aspects help you understand both your own thoughts and feelings and those of other people. You find it easy to express them verbally, in both speech and writing. You think quickly and use your sharp intelligence constructively. Your adaptable nature is useful in unfamiliar surroundings. You also have a flair for picking up foreign languages. Your sympathy for other people makes them rush to you for support and comfort.

Hard aspects indicate difficulty in expressing feelings. Emotions are blocked and confused. You may be very gifted mentally, but sadly you use your talents destructively or superficially, picking quarrels and launching verbal attacks. You also tend to blame others for your own mistakes and shortcomings, or else you cover them up by pointless chatter.

Your worst problems are nervous tension and lack of concentration. You are nicest with people who are weaker or inferior.

MOON TO VENUS   ☌ S

Soft aspects bring profound emotions which you express in an open, honest manner. You have always enjoyed good relations with your mother, which favours all connections with women and family. Basically you're a happy person – gentle, sensitive and sympathetic; quite attractive, in fact. Social life is successful, too. You appreciate all forms of beauty and have good taste and a beautiful home.

Hard aspects can make you cold and unsympathetic, with scant regard for other people's feelings, of which you may even take advantage. You also find it difficult to accept and express your own sincere feelings, and this will cause problems in love and marriage. The cause could be found in your early childhood and in your relationship with your mother. You are self-indulgent and may over-indulge in sex. Your home life is disorganized, and you are generally untidy.

MOON TO MARS   ☌ H

Soft aspects bring powerful emotions and a passionate nature. You're enterprising and courageous and enjoy outdoor life and sports. Your thoughts are profound and you are not daunted by responsibility or quick decisions. You live mainly in the present and are honest and forthright.

Hard aspects indicate frustration, aggression and inner conflict. You are quarrelsome and gossipy, impatient, short-tempered and unbalanced. Very likely you did not get on with your mother as a child. You may provoke scenes and enter physical combat. Generally, you're a nuisance to others. There is a risk of bad health, promiscuity and alcoholism. Family life and marriage won't be without their problems. The greatest success will come to you if you strike out on your own.

174

MOON TO JUPITER   ♂ S

Soft aspects generate love and harmony. You're optimistic, helpful, kind and generous, with deep respect for all living creatures. That is why animals are so attracted to you – and people too, of course! You are calm and confident. All the assistance you'll ever need will come to you automatically. Your vivid imagination holds a creative potential – a literary career is one possibility. Your health is good, and there are good prospects for marriage. Residence abroad is fortunate for you.

Hard aspects bring bad judgement in financial and emotional affairs. You demand too much from your partner and are much too self-indulgent. Although you are kind and generous, you will push your luck and take success for granted. That way you miss out on a lot of things you could have had with a slightly greater effort. You're wasteful and over-confident and blame others for your own mistakes. Foreigners may deceive you, and there may be problems in connection with foreign countries. Scandal is a constant hazard. Watch your health – especially you liver!

MOON TO SATURN   ♂ H

Soft aspects make you tactful and diplomatic. You are patient and ambitious, dutiful and responsible, well worthy of all the trust and respect you enjoy. It is almost inevitable that you obtain an eminent position and keep it throughout your life. Any project of yours will be helped by public support and esteem. Your home-life is secure and well organized. Healthy habits lead to good health.

Hard aspects are an indication of a difficult childhood – problems with or between your parents. Consequently, you have developed into a serious, disciplined, hard-working person with a feeling that you must constantly justify your existence. You may become isolated, lonely, depressed, inhibited and frustrated. Because you don't expect to be loved for your own sake, you will deny love even when it's within your reach. If you could only overcome your negative attitude to yourself, you would go far. Remember that it's up to you to create your own happiness!

MOON TO URANUS   ☌ H

Soft aspects bring an independent, inventive personality. Your life undergoes constant improvements. You need never worry about getting stuck in a rut: stimulation, variation and your own strong opinions will invariably spur you on. You feel instinctively what the public wants and may well exploit this in a lucrative way. You find new solutions to old problems. Friends of the opposite sex appeal to you most.

Hard aspects make you unconventional, if not eccentric. Taboos do not deter you. You may be highly-strung, unpredictable, unreliable or unreasonable. Somehow you're unhappy about your sexual role, and sexual relationships are seldom satisfying. You're quick to take offence and have a violent temper. There are frequent changes of residence or work. Make an conscious effort to become more balanced, and you'll reduce the risk of devastating external events, which you have probably experienced already in some form.

MOON TO NEPTUNE   ☌ N

Soft aspects bring powerful subconscious undercurrents and strong intuition, together with a passive and dreamy nature. Your imagination is extraordinary, and if you use it to satisfy public taste, you could be very successful. You're very sympathetic to others. Charm, taste and refinement are all yours and your life seems to run more smoothly than most. You may even be a parasite, in spite of your high ideals!

Hard aspects bring a confused, neurotic character. You're never satisfied with life as it is and prefer to escape from it in one way or another. Your self-image may be distorted, which will invite a painful awakening to reality. You're unreliable and irresponsible and extremely impressionable, especially when it comes to sex. Indiscretion and ensuing scandal is a great risk. You have strange friends and may experience

problems with the opposite sex. Because you're so suggestible, you must be very careful with any kind of negative
stimulation.

MOON TO PLUTO ♂ N

Soft aspects bring powerful emotions which can affect the lives
of others. Your moods, ruled by your impulses, go constantly
up and down. It is fortunate that you readily accept new
conditions, because your life has a tendency to undergo
sudden, explosive changes. Your circumstances seem to be
always changing – but in the end you'll find that you are
reasonably satisfied with life.

Hard aspects indicate an explosive temper and a domineering
mother in the background. Some kind of traumatic childhood
experience has left its trace. You control others with your
powerful emotions – or you are subjected to emotional
blackmail yourself. Jealousy and envy could easily offend
people and create enemies. Your extreme moods and feelings
could become neurotic. You will either brood in gloomy
solitude or have bitter outbursts of anger.

Aspects: *Mercury*

MERCURY TO VENUS ♂ S

Soft aspects, that is, the conjunction or the sextile, which are
the only ones possible between these planets, make for ease of
expression and discussion where feelings are concerned. You
speak and write with great charm and could be a good
diplomat or author. The arts and cultured social life appeal to
you, since you're both sophisticated and cultured yourself.
You are popular and have many nice friends. Your nerves are
strong and healthy.

Hard aspects between these planets do not exist.

MERCURY TO MARS ♂ N

Soft aspects bring good powers of persuasion. You speak

quickly and enthusiastically; you are forthright and witty and will examine and question any idea you come across, adding your own sensible views. You do very well in the fields of literature and politics. You are sexy, quick at repartee and intelligent. Your partner will show the same traits. You're fond of children but unlikely to have a large family.

Hard aspects indicate a destructive, quarrelsome nature, refusing to accept anybody else's point of view. You're sceptical and unreasonable and often attack others verbally in a vehement, sarcastic manner. Although you are shrewd and intelligent, you will make enemies by pure thoughtlessness. Rash decisions bring a lot of trouble. Anger and frustration will destroy your nervous system. You never admit a mistake.

MERCURY TO JUPITER ♂ S

Soft aspects bring extremely good judgement. You are broad-minded and can see things in their right perspective. Your mental powers can be used creatively – with lucrative results! Your greatest success should come through the professions or perhaps through literature, but you have many strings to your bow. Your ideas are readily accepted by others. You're honest and generous and have a good sense of humour. Travel and new places are lucky for you.

Hard aspects are an indication of over-optimism and a poor sense of reality. You talk far too much and could be insincere and hypocritical, unreliable and indiscreet. Your judgement is bad and you have a propensity for coarseness and rude jokes. You promise more than you can deliver and take on projects you haven't got a chance of completing. Even with the best of intentions you will let cats out of bags at the wrong moment and cause serious problems for other people. Nerves and liver are points of physical weakness.

MERCURY TO SATURN ♂ N

Soft aspects bring a serious nature. You make well-considered statements, speaking slowly and deliberately. You learn easily and like organizing. You're tactful, loyal, diplomatic and reserved and would do very well in an executive position. Good sense, excellent memory and extremely good judgement add to your assets.

Hard aspects indicate a depressed and depressing character. You are timid, insecure and indecisive. Although you may be well-intentioned, your narrow mind stops you from encouraging both yourself and others. You will force your will onto others and can easily become a tyrant. Other people's feelings mean little to you. You're basically limited and frustrated, but at the same time very reliable. You were probably unhappy as a child, and your own children may need some special assistance. You have few friends.

MERCURY TO URANUS   ☌ S

Soft aspects bring independent, original thoughts and notions, which can border on genius, especially in the field of science. You could be a skilful inventor. Your mind is constantly developing; you express yourself and speak quickly. Sometimes your unexpected actions surprise people around you. You have a very good memory.

Hard aspects give a bad habit of questioning and doubting everything, for no good reason. You are tactless, abrupt and eccentric. Even your good ideas are presented in such a provocative manner that you turn potential supporters against you. You're restless, dissatisfied and confused by your misfortunes, which are, on principle, brought on by yourself.

MERCURY TO NEPTUNE   ☌ H

Soft aspects bring imagination, inspiration and artistic talent. You're sensitive and receptive and have deep intuitive insights into other people's character and motives. The same perception you apply to yourself. Your resources are good; you are swift and practical and have many talents. Your dreams could prove prophetic.

Hard aspects give intuition which could, however, be abused to deceive others. You could be calculating, untruthful and dishonest or, at least, devious and unrealistic. Your real problem is lack of self-confidence. You're also extremely gullible, due to a vacillating, fickle, unpractical streak. You may escape entirely from reality into a world of fantasy, dodging any kind of honest work. You may also lose yourself in despair and desolation.

MERCURY TO PLUTO ♂ N

Soft aspects make you clever and dexterous. You miss very little of what goes on around you. Your good powers of perception could make you an excellent psychoanalyst or, coupled with literary talent, an observant novelist. Your concentration is good and could be useful in scientific pursuits. By finding new aspects to problems, you avert nervous tension and worry.

Hard aspects are an indication of above-average intelligence, which can, however, be abused to gain power over other people. You're dogmatic and intolerant, sarcastic and tyrannical, secretive and scheming. Your explosive temper and nervous tension can cause serious problems.

Aspects: *Venus*

VENUS TO MARS ♂ N

Soft aspects make for an active sex life with chivalrous, romantic overtones. You are fiery, enthusiastic, passionate and affectionate and have plenty of sex appeal. Artistic pursuits will find practical application, and you may well have a career in the arts or the beauty industry. It's likely that you marry very early or unexpectedly. In spite of your independent spirit, the prospects for marriage are good.

Hard aspects lead to conflicts in family life, marriage and intimate relationships. You're sensitive and may be treated roughly by others, your father especially. By setting your hopes too high, you pave the way for discontent and resentment. There is also a crude, vulgar and quarrelsome streak. Either you or your partner may be careless, untidy and wasteful. Phychosomatic illness could be a problem.

VENUS TO JUPITER   ♂ S

Soft aspects bring success, well-being and optimism. You're beautiful and charming and lucky in love and other relations. In spite of this, you're not always satisfied with life, but that is to be regarded more as a bad habit. Your taste is refined, with a preference for luxury, elegance and exclusive things. Entertaining or pleasing the public could prove lucrative. Your reputation is good and you will probably live long.

Hard aspects can make you very self-indulgent, wasteful and lazy, pompous and affected. Excess of feeling could endanger your health, and your partner may be a nuisance. Any lies, deceit or treachery on your part will backfire against yourself. Be careful with your reputation and watch your weight. Remember that all your problems are of your own making.

VENUS TO SATURN   ♂ H

Soft aspects lead to marriage with an older or well-established person. Your attitude to love is serious, and your emotions are stable. You're faithful and quite happy to do your duty towards your partner, even if this entails certain sacrifices on your part. You enjoy respect and high esteem and will in due course have wealth and security.

Hard aspects bring a tendency to sacrifice for duty. You may marry late in life or you may marry a person who somehow does not live up to expectations. Another possibility is a partner who is cold and inconsiderate – or perhaps you're the one to show these traits? If you're cold and selfish, you will repel others and become a depressing, unpopular person. You may have or have had problems with your parents – more likely your father – who forced you to assume adult responsibilities much too early.

VENUS TO URANUS   ♂ H

Soft aspects bring attractive, original love partners and an exciting love life. You're lucky in both love and business. Music, literature and drama appeal to you. Coincidence seems to play an important rôle in your life. You have many interesting friends and acquaintances. Your sense of humour and your personal magnetism make you popular, although you guard your personal freedom.

Hard aspects are an indication of weak nerves, due to repressed desires and sexual problems. You have strange friends and may be rather peculiar yourself. You need a lot of breathing space and provoke others with your extreme ideas. Your powerful feelings need a lot of controlling. You have a tendency to cling to a course which will ultimately lead to your downfall, and you stubbornly refuse to discuss your motives. There may be problems connected with your mother, and marriage may end in an enforced separation.

VENUS TO NEPTUNE   ♂ N

Soft aspects bring lofty ideals in love. You have artistic, creative and rhythmical talents plus an ability to write vivid literary descriptions with particular appeal to the readers' feelings. You need beautiful, harmonious surroundings and are mostly to be found in the lap of luxury. You're soothing and sympathetic and love animals. Your health may be delicate.

Hard aspects indicate high expectations of your partner, who will inevitably fail to live up to them. You're not only unrealistic in love but also attract unreliable partners who will take advantage of you sexually. If you could forget your highly strung ideals and love the person for what he/she really is, your relationships would become more successful. But you probably prefer to succumb to voluptuous escapism and erotic daydreaming.

VENUS TO PLUTO ♂ N

Soft aspects bring intense emotions and a strong sex drive. You are basically faithful but your love life can undergo sudden changes – you may be forced to start again. You don't really mind – new conditions could well bring about something better. Another possibility is secret love affairs. Your economy, like your love life, is dynamic and changeable.

Hard aspects give a tendency to intense emotional involvement – if you're not directly immoral, you will mistake infatuation for love and be driven by your desires, with scant or no regard for your partner. You can be very jealous and abuse your attraction to force your will through. If your partner refuses to let himself be dominated, divorce is a likely outcome. There could also be financial reverses.

Aspects: *Mars*

MARS TO JUPITER ♂ S

Soft aspects stand for a born leader – courageous, determined, active and intelligent. You bring out the best in others and inspire confidence. There is seldom any want of money, and for most of the time you're enjoying yourself. Your sense of humour can be a great help. You're broad minded and constructive, especially with things you yourself believe in, such as help to self-help. Your high energy level calls for constant release. Sports should be victorious.

Hard aspects could make you demanding, impulsive and rash. You're unlikely to lack money but you waste it quickly through unwise speculation, gambling or extreme generosity. Your immense enthusiasm and exaggerated optimism could lead to disappointment or deceit in business. Don't be too greedy!

MARS TO SATURN ♂ H

Soft aspects make you courageous, energetic and persistent. You would do very well in an executive position. Your powers of endurance and initiative make you a good pioneer. Skill and ambition will invariably lead to an eminent position. Any emotional stress will be released through hard work.

Hard aspects increase the risk of accidents. You're torn between impulses and caution. Your temper may be violent – you won't accept any opposition and could be cruel, revengeful and deceitful. There is also a tendency to be cold and stern, selfish and cynical. Your energy is uneven – you may suddenly lose all motivation and become depressed. Remember that your only way to success is via hard work and toil.

MARS TO URANUS   ♂ H

Soft aspects will help you go far in fields such as science and engineering. You're ambitious and energetic, intellectual and practical, perhaps with a touch of genius. As long as you can remain independent and follow your own mind, you'll be quite happy to work hard. You are strong physically and very confident. Your problem is an attraction to danger.

Hard aspects make you restless, careless, reckless, nervous, thoughtless, headstrong, impatient and violent. You have an unfortunate tendency to turn others against you. Nothing stimulates you more than a good quarrel, and you could contradict yourself just to set the sparks flying. Life will force you to change course now and then – probably because of your insistence on always having things your way. You are more prone to accidents than most.

MARS TO NEPTUNE   ♂ H

Soft aspects bring idealism – you're happy to help those who are poor or sick. Your physical sensitivity is considerable, as well as your sense of rhythm. At heart you yearn for the unreachable, for things beyond, and you may fantasize a lot about romance or sex. You sense intuitively if someone is dishonest and know instinctively what measures to take in a tricky situation.

Hard aspects can lead to phobias and neuroses and demands for constant sensual gratification. Escapism is always a strong temptation. Attraction to glamour holds a risk of scandal. You are suggestible and may be badly affected by weird experiences. Try to use your vivid imagination for a creative purpose, preferably in fields like dance, painting and drama. You have an insidious streak but may find that pride goes before a fall. Be careful with any kind of drugs or poison and with large animals and brutal people.

MARS TO PLUTO ♂ N

Soft aspects bring a tremendous willpower. You look ahead, never back, and life will force you to start again at regular intervals. However demanding the new conditions turn out to be, it won't be long before you're safe in the saddle again – you're fearless and indefatigable, bold and aggressive, and don't mind taking over the rudder, even in a hopeless situation.

Hard aspects will provoke explosive changes of circumstances. To stop this happening, you may cling to situations in vain. You have a terrible temper and speak with resentment and cruelty. Happiness, according to you, is to be found only on the other side of a confrontation. You're always involved in some kind of battle, since you keep forcing your will onto others. You never forgive a slight.

Aspects: *Jupiter*

JUPITER TO SATURN ♂ N

Soft aspects bring good prospects for success in life. You take care of opportunities and work productively, usually with a fixed purpose in mind. You have good financial judgement and may inherit. In spite of your serious and profound mind, you're at heart quite cheerful and optimistic. You learn easily and may have a special interest in science, politics or law.

Hard aspects imply that you must work hard for your achievements, which will come to you late in life. You find it hard to accept limitations. Occasionally you lose heart and feel overcome by pessimism and depression. You hold on to your hard-come-by means and feel guilty if you ever enjoy any of them. Try to fight your tendency to total despair. The reason for your problems is probably to be found with your father.

JUPITER TO URANUS   ♂ N

Soft aspects bring you an original sense of values. You are forceful, attractive and unconventional. Your refined logic is highly suitable for scientific research and academic projects. You could sacrifice a lot for a cause, and you tend to inspire other people's enthusiasm. They may even subject you to some kind of hero-worship. You're financially lucky and may inherit.

Hard aspects make you extremely radical. You either tell people truths they'd rather not hear, or else you're insincere and hypocritical. No wonder you're not very popular. It all emanates from your own lack of self-esteem. One way to boost it would be to achieve something for a change. Try holding on to your projects and don't give them up until they've been successfully completed.

JUPITER TO NEPTUNE   ♂ N

Soft aspects bring satisfaction without much effort. Your emotions are elevated, and your imagination is vivid. You also have great sympathy for all who suffer. You're happy to contribute to charitable causes. Animals hold a special appeal for you.

Hard aspects imply that your imagination tends to take over from common sense. You keep making excuses for your own shortcomings, such as immorality, deceitfulness, wastefulness, drink and drug abuse, a social behaviour and depravity. At the same time you hate yourself for doing so. If you manage to rise above all these temptations, you may instead attract people with some of the problems mentioned above. They should be avoided, because, in the long run, they would only harm you.

JUPITER TO PLUTO ☌ N

Soft aspects could bring sudden, overnight fame. Your resources are good, and you make rapid progress in a new environment. You have profound insight into other people's character and motives. In adversity you inspire courage with your proud, dignified outlook.

Hard aspects yearn for a violent revolution, possibly with some political pretext. You think the end justifies the means, and you may exploit others unscrupulously. Your own feelings of inadequacy are often covered up by destructive behaviour. At heart you're constantly discontented and frustrated. Only constructive effort will overcome this.

Aspects: *Saturn*

SATURN TO URANUS ☌ N

Soft aspects lead to unusual and considerable results. You combine initiative and independence with prudence and patience. The result is inevitably successful, although the great achievements may come late in life. With a mind that is both inventive and systematic, you have the best possible resources.

Hard aspects give a strange outlook on the world at large. You are violent, unruly and eccentric and won't accept your own limitations. Drastic action is your answer to most things. Nervous disturbance and depression are one risk – physical injury another. You may also act deceitfully and unscrupulously.

SATURN TO NEPTUNE ☌ H

Soft aspects bring good common sense and clear, deep thoughts. You are good-hearted and don't mind sacrificing your own interests on behalf of someone else. You're quite happy to work hard and have a good sense of self-preservation. Your father probably had a good influence on your development.

187

Hard aspects make you unpractical, inhibited and frustrated. You never seem to complete anything successfully. In everyday life you're constantly involved in misunderstandings and confusion. There is also a risk of scandal. Your friends may exploit or deceive you. Your own integrity isn't entirely above approach.

SATURN TO PLUTO ☌ H

These aspects should be seen as a generation symptom, unless they confirm a pattern that has already been established in the chart.

Soft aspects indicate strong willpower and determination. Your work will strongly affect your environment. You may have a deep understanding of life and the world, and a stoical, honest nature.

Hard aspects give difficulty in connection with social affairs. Political or social changes can destroy conditions you have struggled to build up. You may become bitter and disappointed and make great demands on the society you feel has let you down.

Aspects: *Uranus*

These aspects should be seen as a generation symptom, unless they confirm a pattern that has already been established in the chart.

URANUS TO NEPTUNE ☌ N

Soft aspects make you kind and sensitive to other people's needs. You like daydreaming but can also give practical application to ideals. Painting, music or religion should interest you most.

Hard aspects can make you over-sensitive, highly strung and nervous. Reality confuses you, you don't quite understand it. Your ideals are lofty but you lack perspective and a sense of humour. You may devote your life to pointless self-sacrifice.

URANUS TO PLUTO ♂ N

Soft aspects make you courageous, independent and individualistic. If you manage to find a concrete target for your dynamic energy, you will probably bring about some social reforms.

Hard aspects give strong opinions and ideals, usually connected with social conditions, which you would like to reform. However, your rages and your tendency to violence make you destructive, and you seem to pull down more than you build up.

Aspects: *Neptune*

The following should be seen as a generation symptom, unless they confirm a pattern already established in the chart.

NEPTUNE TO PLUTO ♂ N

Soft aspects indicate an interest in hidden and secret things, either science or the occult, and you approach these fields with an objective theoretical mind which will bring positive results.

Hard aspects indicate problems with the social structure around you. You are constantly at war and are fascinated by crime, violence and general destruction. You may also be seriously misled by the occults and should guard yourself against negative stimulation.

5 Interpreting transits

Transits can be tricky to interpret, because they are very much affected by the previous development of the person in question, and also by man's unique ability to question his reactions and further his own insight by decisions and measures constantly taken in daily life.

The following interpretations should therefore serve as general guidelines only. They describe the type of energy set in motion by the transit. Strong, hard transits normally have a discordant effect, whereas soft transits work more harmoniously. However, you can apply your own willpower to alleviate a hard transit and turn it towards its softer variations.

When interpreting transits in *conjunction* with a planet in your birth-chart, softer conjunctions are marked in the list by ☌ S, neutral ones by ☌ N, and harder ones by ☌ H. Neutral conjunctions take on colour from either description.

The following points should be taken into consideration when you interpret a transit:

a) What are the characteristics of the transiting planet? (pp. 37–41).

b) Which natal planet/s is/are activated by the transit in your chart? Which sign are they in? Which houses? How are they placed?

c) How is the transiting planet placed in your chart? (p.73).

For a synastric analysis, go on to page 214.

Description of transits

Transits: *Mars*

Each separate transit of Mars lasts about two weeks but is most noticeable during the three days when the aspect is most exact, and when the planet makes strong aspects to other planets in the world chart.

MARS TO THE SUN   ♂ N

Soft transits increase your self-confidence and energy. You play a dynamic rôle at work – especially if your job is mechanical. Physical and romantic experiences should be pleasant and satisfying, and relations with other people are smooth. You feel well and enjoy robust health.

Hard transits increase your willpower, and you may well get involved in sport, sex or other physical pursuits. You don't mind competition. Impatience, egotism, ruthlessness and anger, however, make you accident-prone. Aggressive behaviour, which may include physical combat, will repel others. Health can also be a problem, possibly due to over-exertion. Don't speculate.

MARS TO THE MOON   ♂ H

During *soft transits* you find an easy, honest expression for your feelings. You enjoy good health, a hearty appetite and a high energy level, and are ambitious and efficient at work. It's a suitable time for sport and athletics. Planning comes naturally and you may take this opportunity to improve home conditions. Relations with women are favoured.

During *hard transits*, the moodiness, slowness or aggression of others annoys you. The slightest thing makes you bad-tempered. Anger and quarrels, especially with women, are inevitable. Try to control your temper and consider other people's feelings. You may experience conflicting demands from home and career. Watch out for accidents in the home, fire in particular. Sexually, you're more aggressive and

191

demanding than usual. Your stomach may be a cause of complaint.

MARS TO MERCURY ☌ H

During *soft transits* you're efficient at work, taking initiatives, solving problems. Ideas are readily expressed and defended, and sport and competitions should be successful. It's a good time for entering agreements and to discuss sexual and emotional problems. Try to apply your ideas in practice.

During *hard transits* you may feel tempted to engage in verbal combat, possibly over finances. You're irritated, snappish and sarcastic with people who don't share your opinions. Rash actions and decisions could cause problems, and you're likely to feel frustrated at work. Don't expect communications to run smoothly. Watch out for injuries, accidents and infections. Surgery may be necessary.

MARS TO VENUS ☌ N

During *soft transits* you crave for romantic satisfaction and become more eager to take initiatives to achieve this. You're more sexy and attractive than usual, so prospects are good. In marriage you experience harmony and fulfilment, and pregnancy can result. Social life is equally satisfactory, as well as artistic and financial pursuits. Relations with women are favoured.

During *hard transits* you become more selfish, demanding, inconsiderate or aggressive in sexual relations, unless it's your partner who shows these traits. Perhaps it's both of you, in which case confrontations and trouble are inevitable. Jealousy and excessive emotions on the part of either side can cause rifts. Waste of money could be another problem.

MARS TO MARS ☌ H

During *soft transits* your initiative and sense of competition increase, as well as your self-confidence, and you feel more motivated to help yourself to attain whatever you want. You're energetic, healthy, competent and ambitious. Any physical pursuits should be successful, especially sport.

During *hard transits* you feel restless and aggressive and make high material and/or sexual demands on other people. People in authority may oppose you. You talk and act rashly, and constant confrontations are inevitable. There is a risk of quarrels, rages and fights, as well as accidents, illness and fever. You may be arrested.

MARS TO JUPITER ☌ S

During *soft transits* you feel optimistic, enthusiastic and self-secure. It's a good time to make plans for the future, to seek adventure or apply for new jobs or promotion. You're more enterprising than usual, honest and sincere, and probably make progress in work, studies or sport. Travel and legal pursuits are favoured.

During *hard pursuits* you may be tempted to over-estimate your chances and push your luck, wasting money, making empty promises and going to extremes in most things. Perhaps you're narrow-minded and dogmatic, fanatically trying to force your values and faith onto others. Your business methods may be unethical, or you take unnecessary risks with speculation and legal affairs. If you're reckless and careless, dire consequences may ensue. There may be problems in connection with foreign countries.

MARS TO SATURN ☌ H

You're cautious but also determined under *soft transits*, prepared to take on more responsibility and work in a well-organized, disciplined manner. The results you achieve are satisfying, and your material security increases through your own hard work. Scientific or mechanical work is favoured.

During *hard transits* frustration and suppressed anger can be the result of hard work and heavy demands from other people. You yourself have little sympathy or consideration to spare for others. There is a risk of conflict with people in authority – you may even be arrested. Try to avoid over-exertion and occupational hazards. Elderly people may be a burden.

MARS TO URANUS   ♂ H

During *soft transits* you crave for liberty, independence and excitement. It's a stimulating period – your social life should be active and interesting: you come across many unusual people and experiences. Your individualistic, creative traits should flourish, especially in connection with science or electronics. It's a good time for trying out new methods at work.

You may feel impatient, restless, changeable and aggressive under the *hard transits*, demanding personal freedom at any cost, without considering other people's feelings. Prevailing conditions make you nervous and you long for a radical change. You turn friends and other people against you. Sudden unexpected events may overthrow your plans, and there is a risk of angry outbursts, accidents and violence, either from you or directed against you.

MARS TO NEPTUNE   ♂ N

During *soft transits* you find it easy to define your ideals and get a creative outlet for your imagination. Your sensitivity increases, especially where music and dance are concerned. You yearn for adventure and a chance to reform your own psychological patterns. Your intuition is stronger than usual. There may be contact with hospitals and institutions.

During *hard transits* you're confused regarding your own standards. Subconscious desires which you may not quite understand are stimulated, and impulses may be difficult to control. Sexual dissipation or deviation is possible. There is a risk of deceit or fraud, either from your side or directed against you, or there may be a conflict between your higher and lower self. Try not to get involved in any shady business deals. Mysterious illnesses, problems with medicines or drugs, food poisoning or alcoholism are other serious dangers.

MARS TO PLUTO ♂ N

Your willpower and determination increase under *soft transits* as well as your efforts at self-assertion and self-improvement. Energetic physical activities appeal to you, especially sport, and you feel more adventurous and efficient than usual. You don't mind destroying the old to make room for something new and better. Scientific research, possibly behind the scenes, is favoured.

During *hard transits* you may be headstrong, egotistical and aggressive, determined to force your will onto other people with scant regard for their opinions. You may be subject to power abuse and domination or else exert this yourself. Anger and stress are likely, as well as jealous outbursts. There is a risk of physical injury and sexual assault, either caused by or inflicted upon you. Be wary of contacts with the underworld.

Transits: *Jupiter*

Each separate transit of Jupiter lasts up to nine months but is most noticeable during the weeks when the aspect is most exact and when the planet makes strong aspects to other planets in the world chart.

JUPITER TO THE SUN ♂ S

During *soft transits* you may experience what is called luck, which is really a reward for past efforts. Your personal development is intensified, and you feel benevolent, generous and enthusiastic. You feel instinctively what the future holds and can make suitable plans. Physical and mental well-being breeds optimism, and you're happy to assist others, who are equally helpful to you, especially people in authority. Even if

195

you don't enjoy any direct success, you can rest assured that you're laying the foundation of future triumphs. All self-improving pursuits are favoured, as well as legal affairs, studies, long-distance travel and relations with children. Pregnancy may well result. Whatever happens, nothing can go seriously wrong under this transit, which gives good protection. Still, try not to over-indulge.

During *hard transits* you may be wasteful and extravagant, insincere and hypocritical. You're over-optimistic, push your luck, over-estimate your capacity and exaggerate in most things. You promise more than you can deliver, and even your apparent kindness and generosity have ulterior motives. Your judgement is bad, you're lazy and may over-indulge in food, drink and sex. Still, these problems are pretty harmless, and any sensible person should be able to overcome them.

JUPITER TO THE MOON   ♂ S

During *soft transits* your moral standards and ethical ideals are higher than usual, and you're likely to find an opportunity to apply them in practice. You enjoy harmony and peace of mind and feel generally at ease. Other people show you sympathy and understanding, which you return. Your economy should be good and your home life happy. Relations with women are favoured, and there are good prospects for pregnancy. If you're planning a change of residence, this is the ideal time, especially for settling abroad.

During *hard transits* you may over-indulge in food and emotions. Your financial judgement is poor, and you may lose money through waste or reckless speculation. There may be conflicts in the family over differing ethical and cultural values. Your need for emotional security increases, but you do nothing to deserve it. The consequence is self-pity for no good reason, emotional dependence and maudlin sentimentality, which may block you emotionally and lure you into making serious mistakes.

JUPITER TO MERCURY ☌ S

Soft transits indicate a good time for making plans for the future. Professional progress is likely, and most enterprises prove lucrative. Take this opportunity to apply for more pay or promotion. Exams should have successful results, as well as negotiations, literary pursuits and academic research. Long-distance travel and contacts with foreign countries are also favoured. You have plenty of good creative ideas and find it easy to discuss them with other people. You develop intellectually and attract good luck.

During *hard transits* you become unpractical, unrealistic, lazy and undisciplined. There can be problems with communications or misunderstandings due to faulty information. Where ethical and cultural standards are concerned, you tend to show hypocrisy and poor judgement. It's an unfortunate time for exams, for starting new jobs or contacting institutions. Prejudice can undermine your plans. There may be problems in connection with legal affairs.

JUPITER TO VENUS ☌ S

Soft transits make you happy and optimistic, generous and kind, considerate, sympathetic and popular. Other people show the same traits to you. Artistic pursuits, economy and love life are all favoured. You enjoy social life and travel. Marriages entered into under this transit are particularly favoured.

During *hard transits* you may become self-indulgent, maudlin, sentimental, lazy, insincere and hypocritical. Your taste is bad and your judgement poor. There may be problems with women. You're wasteful, pleasure-seeking and hedonistic. Travel proves costly, or you could have problems with foreign countries. However, as long as you're aware of the hazards, they are not serious.

JUPITER TO JUPITER ☌ S

During *soft transits* you look ahead with optimism and

197

enthusiasm. Confidence in yourself and life is strong. You probably make an effort to improve your situation, regarding home conditions, family relations and your own character. Cultural pursuits appeal to you, as well as foreign countries and academic interests. It's a suitable time for contacts with law courts, universities, publishers and institutions in general. Take advantage of opportunities to plan for the future, especially where finances, education and personal development are concerned.

During *hard transits* there is a risk of taking on more than you can manage. You over-estimate your own strength or capacity. Be unscrupulously honest in business yourself, anything else will backfire and there is a great risk of deception. Do not speculate. You may feel confused by conflicting ethical and cultural values. Don't be morally hypocritical or sanctimonious in religion. Make an effort to be sincere. Also try to avoid over-indulgence.

JUPITER TO SATURN ♂ N

Soft transits stand for a highly constructive period. You are serious, diligent and determined, applying high ethical standards to your efforts, coupled with a sound judgement. Past labours are rewarded, improving your status and also increasing your responsibility. Professional and financial progress is inevitable, perhaps most noticeable if you're involved with foreign countries or academic pursuits. It's a good time for exams, promotion or pay increases. Support comes from people in authority, and any applications for new positions should be successful. Make plans for the future.

Hard transits can bring problems over money, home life, career, status or legal affairs. Your judgement is not what it should be, and your sense of timing is poor. You may lose your job or experience a crisis at work. Look after your economy and don't run into debt. Perhaps you're drawn between family and career. You compromise and question your own principles – possibly you go through a moral crisis.

Don't expect any support from people in authority. Your reputation may suffer from earlier mistakes.

JUPITER TO URANUS ☌ N

Soft transits will bring opportunities to further your interests – especially travel or cultural pursuits. You're broad-minded, tolerant and benevolent and attract people who show the same traits and will develop into stimulating new friends. Sudden insight may come to you regarding future cultural trends. You're open to new impressions and may find application for a hidden talent. A long-awaited breakthrough could come. Unexpected financial windfalls are also likely, possibly by way of inheritance.

During *hard transits* you're over-optimistic, unrealistic, impatient, insensible and undisciplined. You act rashly and jump to conclusions, evade responsibility and demand personal freedom without considering other people. You want to travel but may experience problems abroad. There could also be trouble over legal affairs or speculation. Don't trust new acquaintances. Try not to promise more than you can keep. Institutions are another possible source of conflict.

JUPITER TO NEPTUNE ☌ N

During *soft transits* your inspiration and intuition increase. Your subconscious becomes a source of sympathy and empathy for others and of increased appreciation of artistic and aesthetic values. Your faith is strong, and solitude and meditation further your personal development. You feel generally idealistic. Any contact with institutions is favoured.

Hard transits make you idealistic – but in an impractical way. Although your intentions are good, you over-estimate the value of your ideals. Don't be taken in by false humility and maudlin sentimentality in others – they are probably trying to pull the wool over your eyes! Or perhaps you are the one to deceive? Disappointment and escapism seem to be the inevitable outcome of emotional dependence and unrealistic daydreams. If you are honest, first with yourself, then with others, you'll fare better.

JUPITER TO PLUTO   ♂ N

During *soft transits* you crave for self-improvement, probably through cultural or academic pursuits. This will lead to considerable progress. You may dispose of old values and make room for new ones. Family conditions improve. New beginnings are favoured by these transits and will bring about better conditions.

Hard transits prompt you to force your opinions onto others, or you may be subject to such presssure yourself. Don't try to improve others but concentrate on your own development! Any religious coercion will lead to conflicts, and family relations are threatened by conflicting ethical and cultural values. In business dealings, any dishonesty will backfire against you. Try to maintain high moral standards. There may be problems in connection with taxes or inheritance.

Transits: *Saturn*

Each separate transit of Saturn lasts up to eighteen months but is most noticeable during the months when the aspect is most exact and when the planet makes strong aspects to other planets in the world chart.

SATURN TO THE SUN   ♂ H

During *soft transits* increased responsibility at work leads to professional progress and, in due course, recognition. Your ideas find practical application, and results are satisfactory. You feel reserved, cautious, restrained and disciplined. Past efforts will be rewarded and old relationships may start again. Marriage to an older or more established person is one possibility. You mature considerably; your patience and endurance will most likely be put to the test. Many people get married or have children under these transits.

Hard transits always indicate a trying period – your vitality is low and responsibilities weigh heavily on you. People in authority or older people in general may make life difficult. High demands made by society prevent you from enjoying life. You may suffer from earlier mistakes and learn some tough lessons. Bad health and depression are common. Neither love, sympathy nor money seems to be at hand. Your own despondency prevents progress. Egotism, coldness and pessimism repel other people, and you meet with the same traits in others.

SATURN TO THE MOON   ☌ H

During *soft transits* you're emotionally controlled and reserved, seriously applying yourself to studies or work. Relations with others are markedly loyal and steadfast. Home life, work and economy are all stable. You may resume contact with women you haven't seen for a long time. Look to your mother for assistance.

Hard transits may bring financial worries and depression. Your environment makes heavy demands on you, and lack of self-confidence coupled with too much responsibility leads to exhaustion and despondency. Other family members offer little sympathy, and you yourself are too preoccupied with your own problems to offer any – you may instead give in to self-pity, coldness and destructive behaviour. An older family member may cause problems or worry. Everyday life is more difficult than usual. You may brood over childhood memories. Try to avoid domestic changes under these transits.

SATURN TO MERCURY   ☌ N

During *soft transit* systematic thinking comes naturally to you, and your work is disciplined and efficient. Important decisions are made and implemented, and plans for the future are made. People in authority are likely to lend you their assistance and support and increase your responsibilities. You are more realistic than usual and enjoy organizing yourself

201

and others. Research and education are favoured. Communications are helpful.

During *hard transits* serious thoughts may turn into sullen brooding, worry and depression. You feel inadequate and may over-exert yourself, jeopardizing your health in the process. There may be opposition from people in authority – you may even lose your job – don't expect progress or promotion. Brothers and sisters, neighbours and friends may also cause trouble. Communications don't seem to function properly. You don't understand others any better than they understand you, so abstain from making important decisions, and don't sign any contracts until the transit is over.

SATURN TO VENUS ♂ H

During *soft transits* you're emotionally controlled and reserved. Socially, you're more formal and stiff than usual. Your need of increased security is fulfilled; love relationships become serious and permanent. An old connection may be resumed, or you fall in love with an older, more established person. Financial support may come from people in authority.

During *hard transits* your emotional life is very restricted. Your own egotism, coldness and lack of sympathy repel others and leave you disappointed, lonely and depressed. You yearn for love but can't have it. Perhaps you have to take responsibility for your partner. Financial worries are another possibility.

SATURN TO SATURN ♂ H

Your powers of organization are good under *soft transits* – take this opportunity to sign important documents and make far-reaching decisions. Professional demands increase, and you mature socially. There seems to be a need for increased material security and long-term planning – you establish patterns for future conditions and find that your status and prestige improve. Older and well-established people are loyal and helpful, and you're likely to reap the fruit of past efforts. You become more ambitious and persevering. Your integrity is above reproach.

During *hard transits* you suffer from worry, anxiety and pessimism. Lack of self-confidence, frustration or external circumstances can all block your development. You feel your responsibilities weighing heavily and may have to take the consequences of earlier mistakes. You may also have to take on responsibility for older people or experience opposition from people in authority. Somehow you manage to make yourself unpopular.

SATURN TO URANUS   ♂ N

During *soft transits* your social responsibility increases. You feel more motivated to realize your objectives, your powers of concentration are good, and progress in science or research is likely. Original ideas find practical application. Personal success comes through good contact with friends and people who share your opinions. Try new methods to live up to the increasing demands made on you.

During *hard transits* you may find it hard to find an outlet for your ideas. Past mistakes may lead to unexpected difficulties which force you to alter your circumstances radically. Friends may prove unreliable and troublesome. You don't trust them any more than they trust you – which is just as well. Health problems are another possibility – bone fractures and nervous complaints especially. At work your habits are irregular. You crave for more freedom than usual.

SATURN TO NEPTUNE   ♂ H

During *soft transits* concentration comes naturally, and you find a psychological motivation for your pursuits. Your mood is serene, and you benefit from solitude and meditation. Subconscious insight and memory bring you closer to your objectives. The arts and institutions are favoured, and so are old connections. Past efforts may be rewarded under these transits.

Hard transits may bring about undefined depression and sadness, caused by subconscious stimulation: you feel worried and anxious without understanding why. Brooding, phobias and self-pity are not unlikely, but the problems of other people bore you. Do not resort to drink or drug abuse. You prefer to evade work and responsibilities but may be forced into secret professional projects. Remember that your reputation could be at stake.

SATURN TO PLUTO ♂ H

During *soft transits* increased professional responsibilities could have far-reaching consequences. Your willpower, determination and efficiency increase. This period could be the end of one chapter and the beginning of another. You may acquire fame through past efforts. Science, research and politics are favoured, and there may be gain through the Stock Exchange or inheritance. New opportunities – possibly unofficial ones – will open up.

Hard transits may bring about a power struggle, and professional responsibility will weigh heavily, particularly in connection with finance. Intrigues and plots cause worry and trouble, and you could be tempted to corruption or dishonesty. Watch out – your reputation is at stake. Mistakes made in the past could also jeopardize your position.

Transits: *Uranus*

Each separate transit of Uranus lasts about eighteen months but is most noticeable during the months when the aspect is most exact or when the planet makes strong aspects to other planets in the world chart.

URANUS TO THE SUN ♂ N

During *soft transits* life becomes exciting and eventful. You want freedom and independence and develop your most original, attractive sides. Unexpected opportunities for friendly and romantic contacts present themselves, and you come across new stimulating people. You're popular and your friends are helpful. Suddenly, there are fortunate chances of realizing your objectives. Your self-knowledge and inspiration increase.

During *hard transits* you may become selfish and self-willed, unreliable and irresponsible. You demand unlimited freedom for yourself, without considering other people, on whom you yourself make heavy demands. You may start sudden love affairs which don't last very long. Your friends are eccentric and troublesome. Divorce or problems with offspring are also possible. Your life may change due to unexpected events seemingly beyond your control. Serious mistakes can be made – don't provoke changes but adjust to circumstances, which are inevitably changing around you. Remember that any dishonesty will backfire against yourself.

URANUS TO THE MOON   ☌ H

During *soft transits* your moods change quickly and your behaviour may surprise both friends and family. Home life is exciting but unsettled. Friends may appear unexpectedly. Women are a stimulating influence. Money may come in erratically and unexpectedly – it's a good idea to use it to improve your home, or perhaps to move house. Your intuition increases and you understand your own motives better. Social life is interesting and satisfying.

During *hard transits* you can be very moody. Emotions are unruly, and distressing events could occur in the family or at work. Women are particularly troublesome, and everyday life is more difficult than usual, partly due to financial worries. Avoid changes under these transits. Your demands for freedom and lack of consideration may repel other family members. Be careful in the home, especially with electricity.

URANUS TO MERCURY ☌ S

During *soft transits* you become more aware and expand your self-knowledge. Your ideas are original and your friends stimulating. Work becomes more stimulating – possibly due to an increased accent on technology. Your intellect is more astute than usual. You're helped by communications and find it easy to express thoughts in speech or writing. There may be some unexpected good news.

During *hard transits* your ideas tend to be eccentric and impractical, lacking continuity. Your decisions are rash and ill-considered. Even people who are normally disciplined and well organized can come across unexpected problems. You're nervous, restless and careless, won't listen to advice and make rash decisions. The result is a loss of routine at work and unpredictable events overthrowing your plans.

URANUS TO VENUS ☌ H

Soft transits are a promise of excitement – you come across interesting new people and may well fall in love. Unexpected gifts or professional offers are not unlikely. Emotions are more easily expressed, and you become more adventurous in love, as your principles stray from convention. You have an intuitive understanding of other people's feelings and needs; your own attraction becomes more magnetic, and you dispose of your previous inhibitions. Objectives seem to come closer.

During *hard transits* you may become infatuated with another person and/or be irresponsible and inconsiderate in marriage and sexual relations. Pleasure-seeking tendencies and a strong sex drive could lead to promiscuity, and unconventional sexual dissipation could bring trouble. Any relationships started at this time will be short-lived due to lack of moderation and high expenses. Eccentric friends could also cause conflicts.

URANUS TO URANUS ☌ N

These transits all indicate a time of upheaval – from work,

family etc. If the *transit* is *hard*, you may find it quite traumatic to adjust to the new conditions forced upon you. You become insecure and anxious when you must look for new directions in life. But unexpected events tend to help you, and in due course you will experience a new kind of personal freedom which you never thought possible before.

URANUS TO NEPTUNE   ☌ N

During *soft transits* your intuition and perception increase and you gain a better understanding of your subconscious. You realize how to achieve your objectives. Imagination can help considerably in seeing what the future holds, for you personally as well as for society as a whole. Gifts and financial gain are likely, possibly through inheritance. Your life may take a sudden turn for the better.

You feel weighed down by responsibility and everyday life and long to escape reality under *hard transits*. You're emotionally confused, lack a sense of direction and seek in vain for a purpose. Your home life is unsettled and you resort to friends, who are probably unsuitable companions.

URANUS TO PLUTO   ☌ N

During *soft transits* your willpower is strengthened and you feel like changing your life radically. Circumstances may prompt you to dismiss old habits and conditions, and you lose old friends as quickly as you make new ones. Your attitude and direction in life may be altered by social or political circumstances. You may discover new socially useful sides to your character.

During *hard transits* your attitude and direction in life change drastically against your will. Don't fight the inevitable but at the same time avoid initiating changes. Guard your economy, which could also change suddenly. You may be forced to accept altered financial circumstances.

Transits: *Neptune*

Each separate transit of Neptune lasts about two years but is most noticeable during the months when the aspect is most exact and when the planet makes strong aspects to other planets in the world chart.

NEPTUNE TO THE SUN   ☌ N

During *soft transits* you're idealistic, inspired and altruistic. Your imagination flourishes, you feel more romantic than usual and experience love in a spiritual way that goes beyond desire and emotions. All spiritual values appeal to you more, and you're generous and sympathetic to those worse off. You could become the leader of cultural projects or work successfully with children under these transits. Your subconscious helps you, and your dreams have a lot to tell you.

During *hard transits* you lack concentration and efficiency, you escape reality and practical responsibilities. You're confused and gullible; self-deception could lead to a painful confrontation with your illusions. Psychological problems are another possibility: brooding, anxiety, phobias or lack of motivation. Be careful with speculation, secret love affairs and excessive use of alcohol, drugs or sex. Unwanted pregnancies are common under these transits.

NEPTUNE TO THE MOON   ☌ N

During *soft transits* your imagination flourishes while everyday life and trivialities bore you stiff. You may gain psychological insight into your own feelings as well as those of others, and you mature mentally and emotionally. Beauty appeals to you more than usual, and you may devote time and effort to improving your home. Rewards for past efforts are one possibility, for honesty and high ethical standards in particular.

During *hard transits* confusion and insecurity plague you. Self-deception could provoke a painful confrontation with your illusions. There is a risk of deception in love or business – either from you or directed against you. Distressing subconscious childhood memories may come to mind. You like to escape reality and withdraw into a dream world. Unless you fight this tendency to unhealthy introversion, there is a risk of neurosis.

NEPTUNE TO MERCURY   ♂ H

Soft transits make you more aware and motivated. You identify your ideals and apply inspiration and imagination to express them creatively. You find it easy to understand your own feelings. Contact with institutions and creative pursuits are favoured.

During *hard transits* you doubt your own ideals; you're absent-minded, forgetful and confused. There is a risk of hypochondria or evasion of work or both. Be careful with medicines, alcohol or drugs, which are all exceptionally dangerous under these transits. You may also develop an illness which doctors can't diagnose. Be careful when driving; abstain from making important decisions or signing documents. Your logic is not working properly; you may be deceived or misunderstood, with serious consequences, or else reveal things that were better kept secret. If you allow yourself to become overly introverted, there is a risk of a neurosis.

NEPTUNE TO VENUS   ♂ N

Soft transits help you understand love in its purest form – you experience sympathy, harmony and happiness in romance. Your contact with other people is very good. Inspiration and aesthetic appreciation are stimulated – a highly productive time for artists. It's also a suitable time to travel and study other countries' culture. Idealistic and aesthetic values are important to you, and you may be spiritually elevated through religion. You're likely to receive gifts or financial contributions. It's the time when you're most likely to meet the person who is your ideal partner.

During *hard transits* you may be deceived, disappointed or disillusioned in love, unless you're the one to inflict this. A secret love affair is not unlikely. You're impractical and irresponsible, over-sensitive and unrealistic in romance. Your subconscious is troublesome and prompts you to escape reality through alcohol and drugs. Speculation of any kind is very risky.

NEPTUNE TO NEPTUNE ☌ N

During *soft transits* you find it easy to understand the feelings of other people. Your imagination is stimulated and your inspiration is a great asset in any artistic work. Contact with institutions should have favourable results. Your insight into life and the world in general becomes more profound.

During *hard transits* you experience emotional distress from your subconscious. You evade responsibility and practical problems and prefer to isolate yourself. At the same time you may become a burden to your family. Abuse of alcohol or drugs is not unlikely. You may also suffer from some illness which doctors can't diagnose.

NEPTUNE TO PLUTO ☌ N

During *soft transits* you explore your subconscious, with improved self-confidence as a result. You may have weird, mysterious experiences, though not without beneficial effects, and obscure circumstances may cause an improvement in your daily life. You find the cause of hang-ups and neuroses and dispose of them. In the process, you gain a deeper insight into other people and society as a whole.

During *hard transits* you're driven by uncontrolled selfish impulses and suffering from the strain of religious or ideological conflicts. You may dominate others or be the subject of domination, and there is a risk of stress or deception. Make sure your motives are sound, because you may be called upon to defend them. Any kind of drink or drug abuse is exceptionally dangerous at this time.

Transits: *Pluto*

Each separate transit of Pluto lasts for over two years but is most noticeable during the weeks when the aspect is most exact and when the planet makes strong aspects to other planets in the world chart.

PLUTO TO THE SUN ♂ N

During *soft transits* you become more self-willed and determined. All your desires are intensified, your sex drive in particular. You yearn for some kind of transformation, which is likely to occur. Old habits and patterns are disposed of, and room is made for new ones. You develop personally and feel your purpose in life more strongly. Money can come from official sources, inheritance or insurance.

During *hard transits* there is a risk of personal or financial power struggles with intrigues and jealousy. You demand a lot sexually and try to dominate your partner. You lack sensitivity and may be too strict with your offspring. Forces beyond your control may bring about a new start in life. If you become involved in secret or criminal projects, you're in great danger.

PLUTO TO THE MOON ♂ N

During *soft transits* your emotions are intensified and your economy is dynamic, to say the least. Women could have a positive effect on both. You long to improve your home life and family relations and may also take an interest in ecology. Emotional maturity usually comes under this transit, and you have a chance to dispose of old habits and patterns of behaviour.

Changes of home life and family conditions may be necessary when the *transits* are *hard.* You will play a dominating rôle in your home, or be subject to domination there (probably by women). Co-operation seems difficult. Financial conditions may change and force you to give up old habits. Deep-rooted psychological problems may flare up. The answer is to break away from your background.

211

PLUTO TO MERCURY   ☌ N

During *soft transits* you become extremely perceptive and intuitive. You hold on to your opinions and won't compromise. This could lead to a break-through, especially if you work in science or communications. Your sound intellectual insight will tell you what course to take – you'll dismiss all the old useless ideas and make room for new ones. Secret information also helps you achieve your aims.

During *hard transits* you may make irrevocable decisions with far-reaching, dire consequences. You dominate others and force your will onto them, or else you're the subject of such domination yourself. It's definitely a critical period in your life. You're suspicious, distrustful and envious. There could be sexual difficulties. Watch out for occupational hazards. Don't sign any contracts.

PLUTO TO VENUS   ☌ N

During *soft transits* you will change your own emotional pattern of behaviour and alter your attitude to sex and love. You gain a deeper understanding of love, which adds to your attraction. You may get married. All impressions make a more intense impact, and artists feel inspired under this transit. You find new ways of utilizing old assets. Your business sense is sound, and speculation should be successful.

During *hard transits* you take little notice of the needs and feelings of others, and at the same time you're selfish and demanding concerning your own. You may use your partner for sensual gratification – or else be seduced or raped. Intimate relations contain some kind of power struggle where either person seeks to dominate the other. Jealousy and manipulation are common. Your sex drive is hard to control. Broken relationships are to be expected under this dynamic transit – but mature people can use it to develop a profound and meaningful relationship.

212

PLUTO TO PLUTO   ☌ N

During *soft transits* your willpower and self-knowledge increase, as well as your intuition. Your understanding of life and the world becomes more profound. You find it easy to dispose of old habits and conditions and pave the way for something new and better.

During *hard transits* you may be forced to dispose of old habits and conditions, and altered circumstances may be thrust upon you. This could call for a tremendous effort at adjustment. Try to accept that this period is the end of one chapter and the beginning of another.

6   Interpreting synastric aspects

Before you start to interpret synastric aspects, assess what kind of relationship you're dealing with: does it involve two business partners, employer and employee, teacher and pupil, parent and child, husband and wife, or two lovers?

When people ask for a synastric analysis, it is usually concerning emotional, marital or sexual relations. Therefore the interpretations have been tailored to suit that type of connection. They can, however, easily be adjusted to fit any kind of human relationship.

When you read the interpretation, bear in mind which planet in each aspect comes from which person's chart. If an aspect is mutual, its effect is, of course, particularly strong, and the smaller the orb, the more important the aspect.

Pay extra attention to any conflicts or contradictions that the analysis may reveal. These are the worst stumbling-blocks in relationships. Also, look out for repetitions from either natal chart, strengthening tendencies and traits already present in each person. And in the same way, qualities from either natal chart can mitigate or eliminate synastric effects.

In synastry the opposition is the most interesting *hard* aspect, because it shows in what areas you have to compromise and work to overcome internal differences. Squares, on the other hand, show conflicts or differences, which you will simply have to learn to live with somehow. When you come across *hard* aspects in a synastric analysis, ask yourself in what quality they appear (p. 49): *cardinal* signs in conflict make for furious quarrels regarding present circumstances; *fixed* signs in conflict indicate opposed uncompromising wills pulling in different directions where the future is concerned. *Mutable* signs in conflict make the couple irritated and nervous, hold them back and reduce their ability to cope with a crisis. Just as in the case of transits, willpower can turn a hard aspect into its softer variation. The elements (p. 52) have a beneficial influence on relationships: Fire signs in soft aspect to each other breed warmth and enthusiasm, air breeds harmonious communication, earth practical and materialistic welfare, and water emotional concord.

The interpretation of conjunctions is marked by ♂ S for softer conjunctions, ♂ N for neutral and ♂ H for harder ones. If a neutral conjunction receives soft or hard aspects from other planets, it can be treated as soft or hard respectively.

Description of synastric aspects

Synastric aspects: *The Sun*

THE SUN TO THE SUN   ♂ S

A *soft aspect* indicates a favourable combination, where you support and encourage each other without infringing on each other's personal freedom. You have a natural understanding for each other, and similar interests and ideals. You're stronger together than each one separately, and you value each other and your relationship highly.

If the *aspect* is *hard*, you may find yourselves engaged in a battle of wills; conflicts are inevitable. You tend to interfere with each other's activities and boss each other around, which causes mutual anger and irritation. The upbringing of children can be a major stumbling-block. If you show each other more consideration, things will work out better. The opposition is a common aspect between husband and wife.

THE SUN TO THE MOON   ♂ S

A *soft aspect* indicates a favourable combination for all connections and especially for romantic and family relations. The Sun person dominates and provides, and the Moon person relies on the partner for security and calm. There is a strong attraction between you; you understand each other's feelings and agree on most issues.

If the *aspect* is *hard*, the Moon person could be emotionally disturbed by the partner's domination. The Sun person is irritated by the partner's sensitivity and passivity. You have problems adjusting to each other and have different ideas about home conditions and the upbringing of children.

THE SUN TO MERCURY   ☌ S

A *soft aspect* makes it easy for you to communicate intellectually. You stimulate each other mentally, and any problems can be solved by open discussion. The Sun person encourages the partner's ideas, and the Mercury person provides good advice. You have many interests in common.

If the *aspect* is *hard*, you have difficulty expressing your ideas to each other, and you may have lengthy periods when you hardly speak at all. The Sun person may be too domineering and the Mercury person too volatile. The Mercury person's ideas are seen by the partner as a threat to authority, and they are therefore generally opposed.

SUN TO VENUS   ☌ S

A *soft aspect* represents an ideal combination for romantic relationships. There is a strong sexual attraction and you're happy together. A deep friendship and mutual harmony develop naturally. You're joined together by strong emotional ties – you understand each other well, and any children you have grow up in a peaceful, loving environment. You share the same values and interests and enjoy social life together. The conjunction is particularly common in happy marriages.

If the *aspect* is *hard*, it won't do much damage, but the Sun person should take care not to dominate the partner too much. You may have difficulty adjusting to each other emotionally. The relationship could be based on sexual attraction rather than love, and breed selfish desire rather than consideration and sympathy. You may also goad each other into over-indulgence, pleasure-seeking and wasteful-ness. Don't pander to each other's weaknesses.

THE SUN TO MARS ♂ H

A *soft aspect* gives a combination which enables you to achieve a lot together and improve your conditions considerably. You encourage and stimulate each other, but be sensible and don't go to extremes. There is a strong sexual attraction, but you are also good companions and may well take an active part in sport and outdoor life.

A *hard aspect* is not easy to live with – it inevitably leads to conflicts or direct confrontations. The Sun person tries to dominate, which makes the Mars person frustrated and aggressive. You compete for supremacy, and this may drive both of you to reckless, ill-considered acts. If either person is weaker by nature and therefore gives in to domination, psychological suffering will ensue.

THE SUN TO JUPITER ♂ S

A *soft aspect* stands for a harmonious combination, based on the same ethical and cultural values, which is a good starting-point for all human relations. You trust each other – for good reasons, as you are kind, generous and helpful, not only to each other but also to other people. Together you are better and stronger than each one separately, and you can achieve a lot with your joint efforts. You strengthen each other's ego and enjoy each other's company.

A *hard aspect* is an indication of difficulty emanating from different ethical and cultural values and/or different backgrounds. You may feel tempted to pretend feelings you haven't got, to fit into a social pattern. The combination is impractical, because you pander to each other's weaknesses. Together you could easily go to extremes, be over-optimistic, wasteful or over-indulgent. An attitude of mutual *laissez-aller* could cause a lot of trouble.

THE SUN TO SATURN ♂ H

A *soft aspect* gives a loyal, permanent relationship. You show each other respect and consideration and are not afraid of taking on responsibility for each other. The Saturn person may take on a supporting, authoritative rôle, which is accepted and appreciated by the Sun person. The ties between you are strong and lasting and probably took some time to establish.

A *hard aspect* indicates a difficult combination. You're tied together by responsibility and duties which you'd rather do without. The negative, pessimistic, discouraging outlook of the Saturn person restricts the enthusiasm, self-confidence and *joie de vivre* of the Sun person. The Saturn person can also feel threatened by the impulsive nature of the Sun person and jealously hold the partner back. You can never let your hair down and actually have fun together.

THE SUN TO URANUS   ☌ H

A *soft aspect* stands for an exciting combination. The Sun person stimulates and is stimulated by the individuality of the partner. But don't try to restrict each other's personal freedom – it is a condition of the relationship. Your situation most likely challenges convention. You may have met under unusual circumstances – perhaps it was love at first sight. There is no risk of everyday boredom catching up with you – even if you lead a fairly normal life, you'll think of some way of keeping your relations fresh and exciting.

A *hard aspect* gives an irresistible attraction which won't necessarily survive. You could cause drastic changes in each other's lives. You're happiest together if involved in exciting and dangerous projects and adventures. In normal life, the Uranus person will become unreliable, unpredictable and rebellious against the Sun person who likes to dominate.

THE SUN TO NEPTUNE   ☌ S

A *soft aspect* stands for an interesting combination where feelings are deep and enduring. You understand each other well and both feel an unselfish wish to give love and affection. The relationship is based on high ideals but not always

218

practical. The Neptune person is sensitive and kind, and the Sun person deals with everyday matters and finds a creative outlet for your mutual ideals.

A *hard aspect* indicates a romantic but troublesome combination, breeding misconceptions, misunderstandings and unrealistic illusions about the partner. Even when intentions are good, the result is bungled. You're not always honest to each other and could encourage escapism in each other – possibly with alcohol and drugs. The Sun person wants to dominate, but this provokes subconscious rebellion in the Neptune person who becomes evasive and irresponsible. The Sun person may become deeply disappointed after having idealized the partner.

THE SUN TO PLUTO   ♂ H

A *soft aspect* gives a dynamic combination with strong sexual attraction and an instinctive understanding of the partner's needs. But if you want the relationship to last, you must both make a point of respecting each other. You develop together and could achieve a lot by joint efforts, especially where your environment is concerned.

A *hard aspect* leads to an explosive combination where both of you battle for supremacy. An intense power struggle with angry confrontations seems inevitable. Only the partner's presence may be enough to enervate you. The Pluto person tries to change or manipulate the Sun person, who rebels against high demands, jealousy and sexual aggression and prefers to be the one who dominates.

Synastic aspects: *The Moon*

THE MOON TO THE MOON   ♂ S

A *soft aspect* stands for a sympathetic combination. You're both very understanding and identify with each other's moods and emotions. You're strongly attached to each other, the family and the home, and share the same values where these things are concerned.

A *hard aspect* means that you must make an effort to understand each other's different feelings and patterns of behaviour, and a certain mutual adjustment is called for. This could be because you come from different backgrounds. You rarely want to do the same thing at the same time. Again, adjustment is the key word.

THE MOON TO MERCURY ☌ S

A *soft aspect* stands for a helpful combination. You find it easy to express your feelings verbally and can discuss any domestic problems. The Mercury person analyses the Moon person who learns to understand moods and feelings better and in return provides a home for the partner.

A *hard aspect* indicates a relationship based on communication only, which may lead to endless discussions about nothing in an effort to cover up for a lack of deeper understanding. You quarrel about home conditions. The Mercury person is cold, logical and critical while the Moon person is moody, super-sensitive and overly dependent.

THE MOON TO VENUS ☌ S

A *soft aspect* stands for an ideal combination. You're united by strong emotional ties, you have a mutual attraction that's both physical and mental, and you find it easy to adjust to each other's moods and feelings. Together you enjoy all the good and beautiful things in life, you're happy in your beautiful home and enjoy the same pleasures. You're indeed a happy couple, harmonious and kind and considerate. Neither of you will ever want for security, love or sympathy. The conjunction is particularly common in happy marriages.

A *hard aspect* gives strong physical attraction – but either person may feel exploited by the other. You can't understand each other's feelings and pander to each other's weaknesses. Misunderstandings are common and you can be very indulgent to each other to compensate for a lack of deeper feelings. You join forces over pleasures and extravagance but little else. One of you may be more involved than the other, or one of you (or both) may marry for security or similar reasons. The relationship is somehow very limited.

MOON TO MARS   ♂ H

Even a *soft aspect* indicates a forceful combination and is not entirely harmless. There is a considerable sexual attraction. The Mars person gives encouragement and security to the Moon person, who calms the Mars person and makes a home for the partner.

A *hard aspect* can be tricky. You keep misunderstanding each other and quarrel over feelings and home conditions. The confrontations can be acrimonious, and if divorce ensues (not unlikely), bitter fights are inevitable. The Mars person is cold, hard, aggressive, crude and impatient, whilst the Moon person is over-sensitive, passive, indecisive and wallowing in self-pity. Normally you ought to repel each other but sexual attraction can lure you to get together in spite of everything.

THE MOON TO JUPITER   ♂ S

A *soft aspect* represents one of the most harmonious of all combinations. You trust each other – for good reasons. Your standards regarding home and family conditions comply. You're sympathetic to each other and agree over ethical and cultural issues. A high ethical level makes the relationship stable. You probably have the same type of background. You're kind and considerate, generous and helpful to both each other and other people. Your home is a nice refuge, but you also enjoy travelling together.

A *hard aspect* could mean that the relationship has an insincere, hypocritical element. You spoil each other and pander to each other's weaknesses. You may also be overly protective to each other in an attempt to cover deficiencies in the relationship. You encourage each other's optimism, over-estimate your strength and like to indulge in food, drink and sex.

221

THE MOON TO SATURN ☌ H

A *soft aspect* gives, if nothing else, a lasting combination. You are loyal and responsible together and rely on each other for security. If the Saturn person assumes a supportive, authoritarian rôle and so deserves the partner's appreciation and affection, the Moon person will mature and provide a home for the partner.

If the *aspect* is *hard* one of you may be a burden to the other, or you could be neurotically dependent on each other. You have an unfortunate depressing, pessimistic, anxious and discouraging effect on each other – there is little warmth between you and you may have married for materialistic reasons. Financial circumstances can further worsen your relations. Even if you're loyal and responsible to each other, it's with a heavy heart. You may use guilty feelings to exert control over each other. The Saturn person is particularly negative and depressing and possibly too preoccupied with a career to have time for a happy home life. The Moon person is moody and dependent.

THE MOON TO URANUS ☌ S

A *soft aspect* indicates a sudden, magnetic, irresistible attraction and infatuation. Your relationship is unusual, exciting and unconventional but not always lasting. Personal freedom, especially where the Uranus person is concerned, is a condition for the relationship to survive. You share thrilling experiences and original friends.

If the *aspect* is *hard* you could make each other nervous and distraught, probably because the relationship demands much of you both in regard to personal freedom, which is difficult to accept, especially for the Moon person. You may pander to each other's immature sides, and your feelings may go up and down continuously. Not an aspect to place your hopes on!

THE MOON TO NEPTUNE ☌ S

A *soft aspect* holds a promise of a sublime combination.

222

You're extremely sensitive to each other's feelings and understand each other intuitively. There is a large measure of sympathy and affection between you. You experience strong emotions together and stimulate each other's sensitivity and imagination.

A *hard aspect* could lead to insincerity. Subconscious emotional conflicts will be activated by the combination, and either or both of you could be a psychological parasite. You could also idealize each other to the point where disappointment is inevitable. You confuse each other and stimulate each other's neuroses, weaknesses and self-destructive tendencies. The relationship could also be secret or socially unsuitable.

THE MOON TO PLUTO   ☌ H

A *soft aspect* gives a dynamic combination with a strong sexual attraction. The Pluto person is the dominating one. The Moon person may find a new life through the partner and experience an important personal liberation. The relationship could be secret and possibly cause upheavals, particularly where the Moon person's home life is concerned.

A *hard aspect* wants to be watched, since it indicates an unhealthy psychological power struggle, to the point of cold war. The Pluto person is determined to control the partner's emotions and stops at nothing. The Moon person, understandably, becomes nervous and distressed and retaliates with a subtle mental resistance which makes the partner furious. A combination to be avoided.

Synastric aspects: *Mercury*

MERCURY TO MERCURY   ☌ N

A *soft aspect* means that you understand and respect each other's ideas and communicate with ease. Any problems that arise are solved logically. You have many mutual interests and achieve good results together, helped by the good advice and information exchanged between you.

A *hard aspect* indicates a controversial combination. You have long, tedious discussions about everything. Your opinions usually differ, and you find it hard to see the other one's point of view. Appointments are often missed and you're less efficient together than each one separately. The main problem between you seems to be a lack of communication.

MERCURY TO VENUS

♂ N

A *soft aspect* means you can discuss your feelings openly, and this helps you through any possible crises. You share an interest in aesthetic and artistic values. You understand each other well and have many friends and interests in common. You bring out gentle and pleasant manners in each other and are kind and considerate together. You stimulate each other's high spirits and sense of humour. The Mercury person helps the partner to understand feelings logically, and the Venus person makes the partner more refined.

A *hard aspect* makes it difficult for you to express and discuss feelings. You may over-analyse and rationalize your relationship on a superficial level, overlooking the more important and profound elements. You may also adopt an emotional pattern which is not genuine and therefore blocks you. A lot of time and money can be wasted between you. You talk rather than act. Your views on aesthetic and artistic values differ.

MERCURY TO MARS

♂ H

A *soft aspect* gives an intellectually stimulating combination. You bring out enthusiasm and enterprise in each other. You're probably amused by games such as chess or bridge – or you may be involved in politics. The Mercury person advises and checks the partner's wild impulses, which may not be a bad thing. The Mars person encourages the partner to act and give ideas a practical application.

A *hard aspect* can lead to aggression. You cannot discuss

224

differing opinions logically and calmly but always end up having angry, meaningless arguments, shouting and screaming at each other. If you suppress these tendencies, on the other hand, you'll become nervous and frustrated. You have an irritating, annoying effect on each other – the Mercury person is indecisive, pensive and critical, whilst the Mars person is selfish, impatient and rash, constantly acting without first consulting the partner.

MERCURY TO JUPITER ☌ S

A *soft aspect* indicates an honest combination. You may have met in a school or teaching situation. You share many ethical and cultural values and interests and find it easy to exchange ideas. You assist and encourage each other and bring out each other's optimism, as well as generosity, consideration and sense of humour. You would also be good travelling companions.

A *hard aspect* means that you encourage projects and ideas in each other which would be better forgotten. You may also be insincere and hypocritical together. Opinions on ethical and cultural values differ, and you could have long, tedious discussions about these without ever achieving any results. You could also misunderstand each other and miss appointments.

MERCURY TO SATURN ☌ H

A *soft aspect* gives a practical combination. Your joint determination is considerable, and you make a conscious effort to realize whatever you've set out to do. You're more efficient together than each one separately and usually do well because both of you are prepared to take on responsibility. The Saturn person is likely to have more experience and discipline, whilst the Mercury person contributes with creative ideas.

A *hard aspect* is not exactly inspiring – you bring out the most anxious, depressed and pessimistic sides in each other. You find it difficult to understand how the other one ticks: you distrust each other and may – quite unreasonably – accuse each other of ulterior motives, particularly where money is concerned. The Saturn person criticizes and demands a lot of the Mercury person, who finds him/herself threatened by the more flexible ideas of the partner and does everything to suppress them. Because of this the Mercury person becomes nervous and finds the partner stupid, dull and torpid.

MERCURY TO URANUS ☌ S

A *soft aspect* gives an exciting combination – you both contribute with creative and original ideas and enjoy travelling and seeking adventure together. Your communiciation is easy, open and forthright. Any joint investigation you undertake will be successful. Interests and friends are unusual and stimulating.

A *hard aspect* shows a tendency to encourage impractical and overly eccentric ideas in the partner. You distract each other and so stop projects from being completed. You are confused and misled by each other's statements. Your tastes differ regarding friends and intellectual pursuits. You enervate and irritate each other. The Uranus person is eccentric and unpredictable, whereas the Mercury person is narrow-minded and nervous.

MERCURY TO NEPTUNE ☌ H

A *soft aspect* indicates a strong immaterial link. Words may not be needed between you – you instinctively sense the other person's feelings, moods and opinions. There is a considerable measure of sympathy, affection and tenderness in this relationship. Telepathy is one possibility. The Neptune person could learn from the partner how to understand his/her feelings and at the same time fire the partner's imagination.

If the *aspect* is *hard*, you can undermine each other and

226

together be impractical, unrealistic and dishonest where motives and intentions are concerned. You may misunderstand each other and miss appointments, probably due to the tendency of the Neptune person to be absent-minded, unreliable and indecisive, or even deceitful and lying. The Mercury person, on the other hand, is prosaic, superficial and insensitive and can't appreciate the partner's romantic, imaginative sides.

MERCURY TO PLUTO ♂ H

A *soft aspect* means that you change each other's attitude to life in general. You encourage each other's personal development and mature together. If you make a joint effort to solve mysteries and uncover secrets, you have a good chance to succeed. You stimulate each other's perception and acuteness.

A *hard aspect* gives a suspicious combination, where you spy on each other and gossip or slander behind each other's back. Your vehement quarrels probably involve money or sex. The easy-going attitude of the Mercury person annoys the Pluto person who wants to force his/her opinions on the partner. That usually has the opposite effect.

Synastric aspects: *Venus*

VENUS TO VENUS ♂ S

A *soft aspect* stands for a highly romantic combination. You have a deep mutual understanding and similar tastes where aesthetic and social pursuits are concerned. You're happy together and enjoy cultural and artistic values. You easily indentify with the partner's feelings and moods. Together you are serene and generally at ease.

A *hard aspect* indicates differing tastes and emotional needs. You cover the lack of deeper understanding by being over-indulgent with each other and by wallowing in false sentiment. Your ideas of aesthetic and social values differ considerably.

VENUS TO MARS

☌ N

A *soft aspect* stands for an extremely sexy combination. Your relationship is ardent, passionate and exciting, but not only that – you also satisfy each other emotionally. Together you're happy, and you enjoy pleasures and social life. Tastes and standards are in harmony. You make each other more resourceful.

A *hard aspect* gives a strong sexual attraction, but it may be selfishly inclined and more concerned with sensual gratification than love or consideration. Often the Venus person has to give in to the Mars person's aggressive demands. There is a risk of jealous outbursts.

VENUS TO JUPITER

☌ S

A *soft aspect* stands for an extremely favourable combination. You are kind, generous and benevolent to both each other and others, and your relationship is lasting and sound. You bring each other joy, luck and optimism, as well as material welfare and social popularity. Your home is cosy, beautiful and peaceful. You support and encourage the best in each other, particularly where ethical and cultural values are concerned.

A *hard aspect* means that you're not quite honest to each other. On the face of it you're kind and sweet together, but at heart you have ulterior motives, usually for financial gain. You bring out each other's hedonistic tendencies and can be very indulgent, wasteful or even self-destructive together. The Venus person may be idle and craving for luxury and the Jupiter person too self-righteous.

VENUS TO SATURN

☌ H

A *soft aspect* gives a settled, permanent relationship where you are prepared to take responsibility for each other and provide the material or emotional security that the partner needs. You're always loyal to each other and good companions. Mutual respect and consideration come naturally.

The Saturn person could be older and more established, and will in that case be cheered and stimulated by the partner.

A *hard aspect* indicates a difficult, cold relationship, which is likely to be involuntary or, possibly, formed with ulterior motives for gain on one side or both. Usually the relationship calls for great sacrifice from the Saturn person, materially or practically, and this often leads to resentment. The Venus person is the dependent one and may find the partner cold, mean, unsympathetic and calculating.

VENUS TO URANUS   ☌ H

A *soft aspect* gives an exciting, romantic combination. The sexual attraction is very strong indeed – it could be a passing infatuation, perhaps following on love at first sight. The relationship is unusual, unconventional and dramatic – you'll never be stuck in everyday routine but constantly part and reunite, with little risk that you'll tire of each other. You like to share exciting adventures and original friends and interests.

A *hard aspect* indicates a sudden, unexpected magnetic attraction – irresistible for the time being but soon past. The relationship could be socially unsuitable. You may also confuse friendship and love. Whatever the circumstances, the Uranus person needs a generous measure of personal freedom for the relationship to have any chance at all to survive. This may be difficult for the partner to accept. Even when your intentions are good, you may mislead each other, with dire consequences, or your most constructive plans may be overthrown by forces beyond your control.

VENUS TO NEPTUNE   ☌ S

A *soft aspect* stands for a sublime combination with a strong idealistic streak: the kind of love which is not self-seeking but spiritually elevated and highly romantic. There is a generous measure of sympathy, tenderness and compassion in this relationship. You may unite in a kind of voluptuous escapism, which renews your bodies as well as your souls.

A *hard aspect* indicates an unsuitable combination which is not recommended. The relationship is often based on false pretences, unrealistic illusions or neurotic dependence. One of you may be more involved than the other and in due course be deceived. The least harmful variety is a confused, maudlin and sentimental relationship, where you find excuses for each other's shortcomings, thus indirectly encouraging weakness of character and self-destruction. Even advice given in good faith may have dire consequences. The Venus person is superficial and insensitive and the Neptune person evasive, deceitful and unreliable, avoiding confrontations at all costs.

VENUS TO PLUTO

♂ H

A *soft aspect* gives an intense combination with a strong romantic and sexual attraction. It's a dynamic relationship which makes you both develop and mature. The Pluto person is probably the leader, whilst the Venus person contributes with charm, diplomacy and refinement.

A *hard aspect* means sexual attraction, which, however, will give rise to an intense power struggle where sex is abused as a weapon, especially by the Pluto person, whose sexual demands are either excessive or abnormal. The Pluto person is also very jealous and would like to reform the partner after his own pattern and, on top of that, exploit the partner financially. The Venus person can either accept this and go under in the process or hold his/her own, thereby risking a break-up.

Synastric aspects: *Mars*

MARS TO MARS

♂ N

A *soft aspect* gives sexual attraction. You're quite happy to take on joint energetic projects, possibly in sport or athletics. You achieve good results together, often professionally. Together you possess an enormous degree of vitality.

A *hard aspect* indicates an aggressive combination and violent conflicts. Even when you agree, you're thoughtless, selfish and rash. You compete, measuring your strength, often with furious quarrels. You both want to be best, and you could goad each other to over-daring, ill-considered acts. Attempts to dominate the partner provoke rebellion. Angry outbursts and perhaps even physical combat ensue. The relationship could be based on a selfish need of sensual gratification.

MARS TO JUPITER ♂ S

A *soft aspect* means that you function well together, and a shared interest in sports and the outdoors is likely. You co-operate at home and perhaps at work too. You may also become involved in politics or charity work. Together you activate and encourage good intentions, combining ethics and energy.

A *hard aspect* indicates a combination where judgement is lacking. You find it hard to accept each other's habits, good or bad. Together you go to extremes – you can be very foolish and waste a lot of money and strength. Over-optimism and opportunism are encouraged, whereas you quarrel over ethical and cultural values. The Jupiter person may be too lazy, self-righteous, sanctimonious and indulgent, and the Mars person can be selfish, violent and crude.

MARS TO SATURN ♂ H

A *soft aspect* stands for a constructive combination. You demand a lot from each other, but in return you achieve good results which help you through difficult situations. The Mars person can activate the Saturn person, who restrains the partner's rash impulses. This increases your ambitions and adds discipline, which works as a good channel for energy. Sometimes it provokes angry reactions from either side, but in the long run you both benefit from it.

A *hard aspect* makes for difficulty in co-ordination. You can't quite decide who is leading and who is following. Any attempts at domination from either party will lead to direct confrontations. You may be joined together in a marriage of

231

convenience. The Mars person is thoughtless and rash and resists the Saturn person's attempts to restrain his/her wild impulses, which are seen as a threat to status and security.

MARS TO URANUS   ♂ H

A *soft aspect* gives a dynamic combination with sexual attraction, where you urge each other on professionally and stimulate each other. There is no risk for being stuck in everyday routines – you share many exciting adventures and have unusual interests and friends. Your objectives, which may be social or political, should be in the same field, and you have good chances of achieving them together.

A *hard aspect* indicates an explosive combination. Together you are foolish and rash, and consequently, nothing works out quite as you had expected. You irritate each other, and this leads to sudden angry outbursts, perhaps even physical combat, usually due to the domineering attitude of one or both of you. Neither is prepared to give in to the other. The Mars person is headstrong and brutal – the Uranus person is unpredictable and unwilling to co-operate. A battle of wills is seen as a threat to supremacy or personal freedom. The opposition here usually leads to divorce.

MARS TO NEPTUNE   ♂ H

A *soft aspect* gives a sensitive combination. You are keenly aware of each other's emotional needs. A secret relationship is one possibility, or joint secret activities. You probably enjoy dancing. The Neptune person could steady the partner and show how greater sensitivity gives better results. The Mars person, on the other hand, can help the partner to give ideals and imagination practical application.

A *hard aspect* stands for an extremely dishonest combination. You don't understand each other and can't adjust to each other. There is a great risk of deception, particularly on the side of the Neptune person, who can't find any other way of defending himself against the crudeness, aggression and

232

domination of the Mars person. You manipulate each other with sex, which plays an important (much too important) rôle in the relationship. Problems arise from a habit of acting without consulting each other. But worst of all is a tendency to bring out self-destructive tendencies in each other.

MARS TO PLUTO ♂ N

A *soft aspect* gives a forceful combination with a strong sexual attraction, but you must make a point of respecting each other's freedom. You intensify each other's determination and spur each other on, helping each other over possible obstacles. You co-operate constructively and can have a strong effect on your environment, possibly working behind the scenes – if the relationship isn't secret, you may well be involved in secret projects. You're happy to compete together, perhaps in sport.

A *hard aspect* indicates a furious power struggle, where both want to dominate the partner, thus provoking reactions of mutual active resistance. You have differing views on finances and career. You measure your strength and goad each other to rash and ill-considered acts or crime, possibly physical combat. If there is a divorce, you can expect bitter feuds in court.

Synastric aspects: *Jupiter*

JUPITER TO JUPITER ♂ S

A *soft aspect* gives a peaceful combination. You have an active interest in and a similar attitude to ethical and cultural values. You are good travelling companions, and home and family life is calm and harmonious. You maintain high moral standards and are probably involved in ideological or charity work. You trust each other – quite rightly.

A *hard aspect* indicates different standards in ethical and cultural contexts, and problems ensuing. One stumbling-block could be different backgrounds. You may pretend a false harmony for the sake of peace or financial gain. You

233

promise each other more than you can keep and rarely achieve results together. Over-optimism, idleness, over-indulgence and waste are encouraged by this relationship.

JUPITER TO SATURN ☌ N

A *soft aspect* gives a serious combination, where you respect each other and bring out the best in each other. You co-operate harmoniously and responsibly, well aware of your social duties. You encourage each other to give ideals practical application. You may work together for charity.

A *hard aspect* means that you question each other's judgment and morals. Activities are not synchronized – you hold each other back when you should push forward and vice versa. You have widely differing political views. The relationship may restrict both of you; if you travel together, there may be trouble, and you usually lose legal battles. The Saturn person is selfish, materialistic, cold, hard and negative, whereas the Jupiter person is impractical, indifferent, weak and indulgent, with poor judgement.

JUPITER TO URANUS ☌ N

A *soft aspect* gives a stimulating combination. You have many friends who bring luck. You encourage each other's personal development and like to take on scientific or humanitarian work, where you introduce new methods. Your home is probably modern and inventive – you like entertaining your friends at home. Original ideas are combined with social broad-mindedness.

A *hard aspect* indicates a wasteful combination, probably based on financial gain. Speculation will be unsuccessful. You love travelling, seeking adventure and having exciting experiences, but these prove costly and dangerous. You may indulge in unrealistic social idealism, challenging and shocking others. You dislike each other's friends and have differing views on ethical and cultural values. The Jupiter person is narrow-minded, hypocritical and conservative, compared to the eccentric, radical Uranus person.

JUPITER TO NEPTUNE   ♂ N

A *soft aspect* gives idealistic combination. Your objectives are the same, and your ethical and religious beliefs are similar. You could work together in an institution or for idealistic purposes. You are good travelling companions – especially if the journey has some honourable aim. You fire each other's imagination and creativity and are sympathetic towards each other.

A *hard aspect* gives an unrealistic combination, where you both contribute to mutual self-deception, encouraging delusions of grandeur and false illusions in each other. Your judgement is poor, and you're undisciplined, sentimental, irresponsible and indulgent together. You could bring out each other's self-destructive tendencies, or travel through life aimlessly in a vain attempt to avoid a confrontation with reality.

JUPITER TO PLUTO   ♂ N

A *soft aspect* makes for a socially aware combination, where you spur each other on to cultural or academic achievements, which benefit society as a whole. The social contribution of the Jupiter person will find a better channel with the help of the Pluto person, who applies willpower and force to a social purpose.

A *hard aspect* gives a relationship that lasts only for as long as it's lucrative for both parties. Each one has financial ulterior motives, and so your opinions on economy, alimony, inheritance or education differ considerably. Together you may be tempted to apply unethical or criminal methods to acquire money or power. Don't speculate together! Travel and law courts are also risky. The Jupiter person may try to indoctrinate the partner with ethical or religious dogmas. The

Pluto person in return tries to force values on the partner, which is encountered with passive resistance.

Synastric aspects: *Saturn*

SATURN TO SATURN   ♂ N

A *soft aspect* stands for a stable combination. Your needs of material security and status comply. You regard responsibility and justice in the same way. You encourage ambitions and self-preservation and are good, loyal friends. Investment should prove profitable.

A *hard aspect* gives an envious combination where you compete between you and see the partner's progress as a threat. But if you try, you could spur each other on and discipline each other with good results. You have a depressing effect on each other and a tendency to bring out anxiety, worry and pessimism. Perhaps your one point of togetherness is your mutual misery and bitterness.

SATURN TO URANUS   ♂ N

A *soft aspect* means that you are good, loyal friends and achieve good results together. It's an interesting relationship – the Saturn person is helped by the partner to overcome anxiety, worry and hesitation and approach life with a more adventurous outlook, which in the long run will improve his situation. The Uranus person is disciplined by the partner, which helps give original ideas practical and sensible application.

A *hard aspect* leads to problems, because neither of you is prepared to compromise. There may be a conflict between political involvement on the one hand and ethical values on the other. The Saturn person is old-fashioned, anxious, materialistic and negative, and the Uranus person impractical, unreliable, radical and eccentric.

SATURN TO NEPTUNE ☌ H

A *soft aspect* gives plenty of patience and understanding. Speculation should prove profitable. You may be engaged in secret activities or joint financial projects – with good results. The Saturn person stabilizes the partner mentally, and the Neptune person makes the partner less materialistic and more refined.

A *hard aspect* indicates a psychological blockage which stands in the way of sympathy and understanding. You have a depressing, pessimistic effect on each other, and the atmosphere around you is emotionally unhealthy. Either of you could exploit the other financially. Confusion and misunderstandings are only to be expected – possibly due to the Neptune person's lack of discipline and responsibility. The Saturn person regards the partner's subtleness and sensitivity as neurotic, whereas the Neptune person sees the partner as cold, narrow-minded and materialistic.

SATURN TO PLUTO ☌ N

A *soft aspect* stands for a durable relationship where you're happy to take on responsibility and discipline and co-operate to improve yourselves and your environment. You may work on joint business projects, possibly secret ones. Politics is another possible field for you.

A *hard aspect* leads to mutual distrust and a power struggle. You are both most concerned with personal profit – money or status – and can be drawn into intrigues, crime or courtcases. A divorce would be acrimonious. The Saturn person's status and security are threatened by the partner's unreliable, anarchistic attitude.

Uranus, Neptune, Pluto

Internal aspects between these planets apply to whole generations and have no great personal significance. Aspects formed by these planets to the others are listed under the other planets.

Instructions for drawing up the birth-chart

Here is a picture where you can draw up your own birth-chart, using the information on your data card. The sample chart on p. 57 can be used for reference.

Start with the sector to the extreme left in the circle. In the outer part of this sector, you insert the symbol of your Ascendant sign (♒ in the sample chart). A key to all the symbols for planets and signs is provided on p. 34. Then you insert the other sign symbols counter-clockwise, in their normal sequence, as shown in the sample chart.

From the beginning of the Ascendant sector (top to bottom, i.e. counter-clockwise), you count the degree of your Ascendant (4° in the sample chart). Mark the Ascendant with an arrow pointing from the outer periphery and with the letters Asc. and the degree given on your data card. In the same way, mark the point of the Descendant in the opposite sector with the same degree (counted bottom to top, i.e. counter-clockwise) and a bar from the outer periphery. The axis between these two points on the periphery, the horizon of the chart, is then drawn out – but only in the inner circle, through its centre-point.

Now go to the sector marked with the sign of your Midheaven (♐ in the sample chart). Count the degree of your MC, counter-clockwise from the start of the sector, and mark it with an arrow, the letters MC and the degree (5° in the sample chart). Right opposite you mark IC with a bar and the same degree.

Then you insert the symbol of each planet in its proper place. Each sign sector measures 0°–30°, counted counter-clockwise. Indicate the exact position of each planet with a cross-bar on the inner periphery and the degree in the outer part of the sector.

Finally, draw out the house cusps as given on the data card. Only the houses below the horizon are specified, since they correspond to houses of equal size above the horizon. The

238

cusp diagonals should be drawn in the inner circle only, from one point on the inner periphery through the centre of the circle to its opposite point. House I, like House VII, starts out from the horizon. House X equals the MC, house IV the IC. The degrees of the house cusps are inserted outside the outer periphery, so as not to confuse them with the degrees of the planets.

Last of all, you mark the numbers of the houses: I to XII in the middle of the circle, counter-clockwise from the Ascendant.

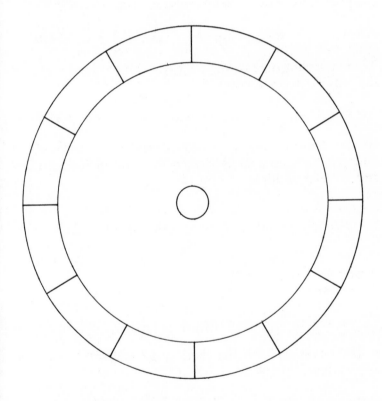

Suggested reading

American Astroanalysts Institute: *Astro-analysis* (Corgi, 1976)
Twelve comprehensive volumes, one for each Sunsign, with general astrological information as well as simplified tables and interpretations of planetary positions and aspects.

Arroyo: *Astrology, Psychology and the Four Elements* (CRCS, 1975)
A book dealing mainly with the psychological implications of the four elements in astrology.

Arroyo: *Astrology, Karma and Transformation* (CRCS, 1978)
A book dealing mainly with the profound mental and spiritual effect of the outer planets of transformation on the individual and his relationships.

Carter: *Astrological Aspects* (L. N. Fowler, 1930)
In-depth interpretation of each possible natal aspect.

Carter: *The Principles of Astrology* (The Theosophical Publishing House, 1925)
A profound definition of the astrological concepts.

Cunningham: *An Astrological Guide to Self-Awareness* (CRCS, 1978)
A book dealing with the therapeutic and self-therapeutic application of astrology.

Getting: *The Book of the Zodiac* (Hamlyn, 1972)
A description of the twelve astrological principles, historically documented and well illustrated.

Goodman: *Sunsigns* (G. Harrap, 1968)
A comprehensive, accessible description of the twelve Sunsigns.

Horoscope magazine, 1977–82
A monthly magazine containing many interesting articles on various astrological themes, as well as monthly forecasts.

Mayo: *Teach yourself astrology* (English Universities Press, 1964)
A textbook explaining the general concepts of astrology and teaching the technicalities of horoscope-casting.

Michelsen: *The American Ephemeris for the 20th Century* (Astro Computing Services, 1980)
A book listing the detailed position of each planet, day by day, 1900–2000.

Meyer: *A Handbook in Humanistic Astrology* (Anchor Books, 1974)
A fairly advanced book concentrating on the humanistic aspect of astrology.

Neugebauer: *The exact sciences in antiquity* (Brown University Press, 1951)
A thesis describing the origins of astrology and other ancient sciences.

Parker: *The Complete Astrologer* (Mitchell Beazley, 1971)
A comprehensive work for the ambitious student of astrology, including every possible aspect of the subject.

Joan Quigley: *Astrology for Adults* (Holt, Rinehart & Winston, 1969)
A book giving detailed interpretations of the different planetary positions.

Sakoyan/Acker: *The Astrology of Human Relationships* (Peter Davies, 1976)
A book listing detailed interpretations of all possible synastric aspects.

Sakoyan/Acker: *Predictive Astrology* (Harper & Row, 1977) A book listing detailed interpretation of all major transits.

Understanding Astrology (Octopus, 1973)

The following booksellers stock astrological books:

W & G Foyle Ltd,
119 Charing Cross Road,
London WC2.
Tel.: 01-437 5660.

Atlantis Bookshop Ltd,
49a Museum Street,
London WC1.
Tel.: 01-405 2120.

Compendium Bookshop,
240 Camden High Street,
London NW1.
Tel.: 01-485 8944.

Hollywood Road Bookshop,
8 Hollywood Road,
London SW10.
Tel.: 01-352 4659.

Emergence,
75 Sutton Court Road,
Chiswick, London W4 3EQ.
Tel.: 01-994 8976.

Kensington Bookshop,
140 Kensington Church Street,
London W8.
Tel.: 01-727 0544.

Odyssey,
30 Lambs Conduit Street,
London WC1N 3LE.
Tel.: 01-405 7635.

Watkins,
21 Cecil Court,
Charing Cross Road,
London WC2.
Tel.: 01-836 2182.

Astrological Organizations:

The Astrological Association,
Membership Secretary: Dick Llewellyn,
Bay Villa,
Plymouth Road,
Totnes, Devon TQ9 5PQ.

The Astrological Lodge,
c/o Maggie Hyde,
18 Northcote Road,
St. Margaret's,
Twickenham,
London.

The Faculty of Astrological Studies,
2 Four Acres, Holden Road,
London N12.

The Centre for Astrological Counselling,
48 Porchester Terrace,
London W2 3TP.
Tel.: 01-723 1140.

Index